MINDFULLY INCLINED:

Reports from the Path Toward Wisdom and An Open Heart

Kay M. Davidson, Ph.D.

The essential human calling:

progressively unveiling the sun in our heart

John Welwood

Contents

PREFACE

When I was first exposed to meditation and mindfulness 30 years ago, neither my research background in graduate school nor my training as a psychologist went out the window. I not only became a practitioner of meditation and mindfulness, I studied it, I wrote about it, I thought about it from the perspective of a therapist, and I took courses to teach it. It has been a surprise to me that, given how long I have been involved in this arena, I have not tired of learning more, I have not forsaken sitting, I have continued to attend retreats. In other words, I have not only found the lessons I've learned to be valuable, but I have also discovered that there is no end to the possibilities that this path has offered me personally. Moreover, I have come to believe, on only a slightly larger scale, that all human life would be better served if these principles and practices were a part of a global ethos.

As of 2023, there are many excellent teachers of this material available to everyone through podcasts, on-line courses, and retreats. Some of them who have contributed greatly to my path will be mentioned as I go along. And there are many excellent books available by those teachers. The public domain belongs to them.

But I have asked myself if there was something I wanted to do with the experiences and understandings that have come to me as I've lived with and into these teachings over the years. In attempting to answer that question, I began to go through the materials I have accumulated - - writing, teaching, journaling - - to see what, if anything, would emerge. It has been an instructive exercise. What really hit me was how valuable and necessary these practices have been to me. They have been with me and served me well as I navigated a cancer diagnosis, my mother's aging and death, and marital issues. And it has become clear to me through this process that even though my journey of becoming more awake to this life is not like anyone else's, in some ways, because it is a human life, some of it will be like everyone else's journey.

It is my belief that meditation and mindfulness offer the practitioner the means to access our better natures, even when under the stresses of daily life. When my husband and I were active mindfulness teachers, we had formed the explicit intention to aim our offerings toward living with more ease in this life. That's the gist of the pieces that I've included in the pages that follow.

What I have put together is neither chronological nor a neat progression toward becoming more mindful. It is a mix of pieces about what it's been like for me over 3 decades on this path and how mindfulness practices have contributed both to easing the difficult times and increasing the joyful ones. Sometimes, it involves insights. Sometimes, it reveals frustrations, sometimes, it offers teachings. Hopefully, it's always real.

<u>In Any Event</u>
If we are fractured
we are fractured
like stars
bred to shine
in every direction,
through any dimension,
billions of years
since and hence.

I shall not lament
the human, not yet.
There is something
more to come, our hearts
a gold mine
not yet plumed,
an uncharted sea.

Nothing is gone forever.
If we came from dust
and will return to dust
then we can find our way
into anything.

What we are capable of
is not yet known,
and I praise us now,
in advance.
                    Dorianne Laux

Do not go by revelation or tradition,
do not go by rumor, or the sacred scriptures,
do not go by hearsay or mere logic,
do not go by bias towards a notion or
by another person's seeming ability
and do not go by the idea 'He is our teacher.'

But when you yourself know that a thing is good,
that it is not blamable,
that is praised by the wise
and when practiced and observed
that it leads to happiness,
then follow that thing.
The Buddha

THE BEGINNING

The Opening

The Summons

Resonance

The Opening

It was about 30 years ago that I was sitting on an uncomfortable stool in the gallery of Indian art at the Virginia Museum of Fine Arts. There were 30 or 40 others similarly seated, listening to a professor of Eastern religions talk about the meaning held by the sculpture that surrounded us. He was saying that art in Hindu temples - - the origin of the pieces in the gallery - - was meant to house temporarily the spirit of the god personified in the sculpture. A worshipper would confront the image, invoke the spirit through ritual and then beseech the power of that particular deity. He noted that each of the many figures in the gallery served a different purpose, and, through the devotions of the worshipper, each became a vehicle for specific spiritual energies. The imagery, to my Western eyes, was odd, even fantastical. Many figures were multi-armed, some animal-headed, some emaciated and fierce-looking, while others were distinctly sensual. What had they to do with the divine? How could they serve a worshipper's spiritual needs?

There then came a moment in the lecturer's presentation when he described the Hindu concept of the Ultimate or the Absolute, the all-permeating Divine Principle. In the Hindu tradition, he said, the Ultimate was believed to be far beyond our human ability to grasp; by its very nature, it transcended mundane understanding. The sculpture in the gallery, then, only represented aspects of that which in its totality could not be captured or known.

The odd appearances - - four arms, elephant heads, voluptuous bodies - - conveyed the mythical prowess and 'more-than-human' features of the gods, but no one of them was the Ultimate. In this view, then, the Absolute was the sum of and far more than the sum of every Hindu divinity. The Hindu pantheon was populated by thousands of gods and goddesses, many more than were present in the museum's gallery.

It was in this moment, in this gallery, among this group of thirty or forty, that I was suddenly given a glimpse of the Divine. I looked around me, and I "saw" each human embodiment there, just as with each sculptural embodiment, as an aspect of the Divine; I "knew" that each of us carried a spark of the Ultimate within and that not only each of us in that space, but every human everywhere carried that treasure; and I understood that the Ultimate, which some call God, was the sum of and beyond the sum of each of our embodied sparks.

In the experience of that knowing, I felt a freedom of Spirit that was new to me. Liberating. Expansive. I became aware that I, too, was a spiritual being. I, too, could connect with the transcendent - - because I just had.

With this briefest of glimpses into my connection with the Ultimate, my "the groping toward wisdom" (Jung) began. As it happened, I later discovered in that same museum a deep resonance with Buddhism. Though at the time, I knew no one else who was Buddhist, and though I had never read about Buddhist thought, so much of what I began to learn through the study of its art not only made sense but touched my heart as well. It has been so ever since.

It was not by accident that the meeting between me and the transcendent took place in a museum gallery. Nor that the study of Buddhism led to the discovery of my spiritual path- that of meditation and mindfulness. Those meetings were among the 'causes and conditions' that paved the path. And, while moments of awakening, of transformation, can occur anywhere at any time, what each of us brings to meet those moments - - our history of experiences, our unique personal dispositions - - are determining factors. The horizontal conventional axis of our lives matters; its colors particularize our spiritual experiences. Just as each sculpture in the gallery houses certain spiritual energies, so do we.

The odd-looking deity, Ganesha, whose image appears at the head of this piece, has something to say about this realm of beginnings. Among Hindus, he is known as the Lord of New Beginnings, and Ganesha is invoked whenever a venture is undertaken; he is also the guardian of thresholds and is often depicted in sculpture at the entrance to temples in India as a symbol of transition from the secular domain to the sacred. In a sense, he serves as a reminder that with every beginning, there is a move from one territory to another, a crossing to a different space.

The Summons

A close encounter with a Buddhist image marked a significant moment in my mindfulness journey. This took place in the 1990s during the time that I was leading tours as a docent at the Virginia Museum of Fine Arts (VMFA). The museum had opened an exhibition of a recently acquired collection of Himalayan and Nepalese art, and docents were being trained to offer tours of the collection. I had a day job then as a clinical psychologist in private practice; serving as a docent was a way to give my heart and mind a bit of relief from the sometimes intense demands of that day job. As it turned out, though, becoming a docent had given me far more than relief. It created an internal opening that eventually led to expanding my view of our human experience, and it further offered me the means to live my life more fully. It had brought me to meditation and mindfulness.

That first close encounter was with Yamantaka, an important Tibetan Buddhist deity. The VMFA's version of this deity is sculptural and prepossessing. Intimidating. He is a six-faced being, more than four feet tall, carved in wood, with a set of bulging eyes; each of his 34 arms holds a weapon, and each of his 16 legs stands on the body of an animal or demon. He has a fierce countenance, and his many-limbed body and array of weapons represent his unearthly power to overcome all obstacles to spiritual awakening. In one hand, for example, he raises a chopper, a bladed instrument that can cut through anything that stands in the way of a believer's enlightenment. In another, he holds a lasso to gather a practitioner's discursive thoughts.

When I learned of Yamantaka's attributes, my psychologist's orientation was alerted. I certainly had experienced discursive thinking myself and had sat with many clients whose thoughts would not give them any peace. I recognized that this Buddhist perspective knew something about our very human minds. I read that the Buddhist perspective considered anger to be like holding a hot coal in one's hand with the intention of throwing it at another and then asking, "Who is hurt here?" I knew that a belief system cultivating that understanding was something I wanted to learn more about.

My curiosity was aroused.

Resonance

Inspired by Tibetan Buddhist art, I began my instruction in meditation and mindfulness in the 1990s via audio tapes by teachers Sharon Salzberg and Joseph Goldstein. I also found a local teacher who had a personal connection to the Insight Meditation Society (IMS) in Barre, Massachusetts, the home of both Salzberg and Goldstein. It wasn't long before I spent two weeks in Barre, first at the Barre Center for Buddhist Studies, learning about the Abidharma, a foundational Buddhist text, then moving next door to IMS for a ten-day silent retreat.

Those were a challenging two weeks: challenging because there was so much scholarship to absorb and challenging because my mind and body struggled with so much silence. I was perpetually uncomfortable until the last few days of the retreat, and I was surprised by the depth of the loneliness I felt among the 100 other meditators. Yet, there was something I loved about both experiences.

I was later asked by a meditation teacher about what had sparked my interest in Buddhism in the first place. She told me that many came to Buddhism through the path of suffering. Was this true of me as well? I replied that no, it was not. I had been fortunate in that no difficult life experiences had motivated my exploration. Rather, I answered, upon my exposure to the Buddhist worldview and the principles of its practices, I had felt a "resonance" to them at a deep level of my being. The ideas seemed to fit me; they rang true for me in a way that other belief systems never had. And, as I was to learn, Buddhism is all about the experiencing of its beliefs through practice so that an individual can then discern for herself what is true. That, too, resonated with me.

Jungian James Hollis speaks of resonance this way:

When something is of us, is for us, it sets off a tuning fork inside us. It resounds because it has always been there…The resonance within us cannot be willed; it happens…

There is, then, something of ourselves to be learned in every experience of resonance. Discovering the nature of that something helps put us more in tune with ourselves and, sometimes, more in tune with the universe, in harmony with its heartbeat. At least, that was true for me. The reciprocal of the relationship with resonance is in the revelation of what is ours to name and to bring to light what in the world each of us can make known in a way that no other being can make known. It invites us to participate in the unfolding not only of ourselves but also in the evolution of the universe. In that light, resonance and the curiosity it aroused in me led to my teaching and to the writing of these words.

Resonance, says Hollis,

> *is the surest guide to finding our own right path. It constitutes an inner guide amid the imposing images of the outer world and the constant traffic of the intrapsychic world…To hear it, one must be attentive, faithful, courageous enough to break from the power of the other cacophonous sounds and hear the resounding of our soul's intent.*

Whether we 'resonate' with the word 'soul' or choose, as I do, a different phrase like 'inner wisdom,' Hollis reminds us that we have to be quiet enough to hear that resonance. That is a powerful argument for meditating, for intentionally visiting our inner life so that we can listen for the guide to our own right path…

<u>The Dakini Speaks</u>
My friends, let's grow up.
Let's stop pretending we don't know the deal here.
Or if we truly haven't noticed, let's wake up and notice.
Look: Everything that can be lost will be lost.
It's simple - how could we have missed it for so long?
Let's grieve our losses fully, like ripe human beings,
But please, let's not be so shocked by them.
Let's not act so betrayed,
As though life had broken her secret promise to us....
Let's stop making deals for a safe passage:
There isn't one anyway, and the cost is too high.
We are not children anymore.
Jennifer Welwood

REALITY CHECK: How Things Are for You and Me

The Realities Of Life

    No Immunity

    The Truth Of Change

    Uncertainty

    Flexibility Of Being

Trees And The Four Conditions

    The First Condition: Our Evolutionary Heritage

    The Second Condition: Our Genetic Heritage

    The Third Condition: Our Family Of Origin

    The Fourth Condition: Social And Cultural Norms

Awareness

The Realities Of Life

While this collection of essays is not explicitly about Buddhist thought and practice, it is written by and is sometimes about a person(me) whose beliefs, attitudes and behaviors have been deeply imprinted by Buddhist thought and practices. Some of the content directly or indirectly refers to and is based on Buddhist principles, as is the origin of mindfulness itself. Since the initial teachings of mindfulness 2500 years ago, time and cultures have left their impacts on how mindfulness has evolved so that it is now practiced, at least in the West, with a more secular orientation. That is how these pages are oriented as well. It should be noted that this collection is by no means a thorough exploration of the many facets of mindfulness or meditation. It is only reflective of one person's engagement with this complex subject matter.

That said, an important group of fundamental understandings taken directly from Buddhist teachings serves as the underpinning of mindfulness as well as the pieces in this collection - - understandings having to do with the realities of our human existence. Meditation teacher Christina Feldman names these realities 'the Unarguables;' Buddhist scriptures call them 'the three marks of existence.' Teacher Ruth King describes them as life's Three Ps: Its not perfect, its not permanent and its not personal. Each of those wisdom sources refers to the given and unchangeable truths that are a part of being alive in the world. Everyone and everything is subject to these truths. These are:

The truth of suffering. There is distress. Life holds pain, illness, aging and death as well as the dissatisfaction that life does not comply with our desires. (It's not perfect.)

The truth of impermanence. All things change. Nothing stays the same. (It's not permanent.)

The 'self' we believe ourselves to be is a constantly shifting, ungraspable coalition of causes and conditions. If everything is impermanent, so am I. (And it's not personal)

While the deepest understanding of these 'realities' is said to lead to ultimate wisdom and insight into the nature of existence, that pursuit may not be the aspiration for many of us. I, for one, am not expecting to reach that 'nth' degree of understanding. However, through the practices of meditation and mindfulness, I have come to a clearer and less resistant relationship with each of them because circumstances in my life have underscored their reality.

No Immunity

Several years ago, I was listening to one of Tara Brach's podcasts. Tara is the founder of the Insight Meditation Community of Washington and the author of several books. This was a podcast of one of her Wednesday night classes at IMCW when she dedicated some time for a Q&A. A young man came up to the mike in this roomful of several hundred people and said something like,

"I've been smoking a lot of weed lately (and this was well before the legalization of marijuana), and sometimes I prefer being high to being with people, and I'm getting a lot of grief about that from my friends, and I'm not sure I want to stop."

The room was fully attentive, waiting to hear Tara's response. She began her comments simply. "Thank you for being real. It matters."

One of the things that has drawn me to mindfulness and meditation practices is that realness and that acceptance of the realness that Tara communicated. In her response, she wasn't condoning this man's marijuana habit, nor was she condoning the fact that he chose getting high over his relationships; what she thanked him for was his willingness to acknowledge and speak what was real for him in that moment.

Being real matters. It matters because life is hard. And sometimes it's very hard. When people we love suffer, when we struggle with a painful past when our work situation piles on stress after stress, when our child is in trouble and on and on. So why not do what we can to avoid or escape our pain - - like smoking a lot of weed?

I titled this "No Immunity" because, as one writer has said, none of us is immune to being asked to cope with what we never asked for, with what we deeply, deeply did not want. As a long-time meditator, I have found the practice of being with what s real, of turning toward the difficult rather than attempting to escape what is hard, to be among the two practices that have been the most impactful on my life. I can say that because the benefits have been so obvious at such big moments: when in the midst of my own serious illness and feeling the fear, practicing enabled me to be with it without becoming overwhelmed by it (fear is not a good place to come from when making medical decisions); when caring for my mom for the two years following her stroke, I felt frustrations with the medical community and sometimes with her, but my practice allowed me to deal calmly with the hospitals and to choose to come from compassion with my mother; then with her as she was dying, allowing my grief and my exhaustion enough time so that I could be with her in love. It helped me live not only a more authentic life but has opened me to deeply meaningful experiences. Not to mention giving me more confidence in my capacity to deal with the unexpected and handle conflict in my marriage more like a grown-up.

It has helped me. A lot.

Attending retreats has played a major role in the slow development and strengthening of that capacity for allowing and staying with unpleasant experiences. Consider, for a moment, what happens when we choose to sit in silence. What's the first thing we notice? Likely, we notice that our thought machine is at work, generating its product a mile a minute. For many of us, it can be uncomfortable to be with that busy mind. In fact, as an interesting research study found, 67% of men and 25% of women preferred to give themselves a painful electric shock rather than sit in silence with their thoughts. The silence was too unpleasant. And, as many of the volunteers in that study chose to do, their reaction to that unpleasantness was to turn away, to find something to distract them, to shift them away from the internal experience they were having. That is avoidance. At a retreat, when the silences are longer and more frequent, just by sitting there meditating in the quiet, we are offered a window into what we do when something unpleasant is happening.

Meditation teacher Jack Kornfield, who spent time as a monk in Thailand, has written, "In certain temples there, I saw this prayer: May I be given the appropriate difficulties so that my heart can truly open with compassion." In a way, that's what happens on retreat or when we meditate regularly. We are asking to learn about what's in there, what we carry around with us. This idea is reflected in the saying, "No mud, no lotus." The symbolic lotus flower blooms out of the mud; its growth is rooted in the dirt and grime. As the metaphor goes, it is from suffering that we learn compassion, from loss that we learn understanding, and from overcoming struggles that we come to discover our own strength and beauty. These struggles may just be the 'appropriate difficulties' that we need in order to grow.

'Appropriate difficulties' almost always arise on retreat. The invitation when something does come up is to check out our level of willingness to be with it. If it's a moderate discomfort, for example, I might ask myself if it's possible to stay with it for a while and bring some curiosity to it.

Teacher Ruth King:

We allow what's here because it is what's here. It's like fine-tuning a radio station to rid the static of resistance or fear so that clarity pierces through. When we allow what's here, our energy is freed. It's not about fixing a problem. Allowing supports us in touching and letting go of the resistance to what's here - - the good, the bad and the ugly. We don't have to love what is happening to allow. We are simply making space for what is already here. To allow is to soften.

We ask ourselves if we're willing, and if we are, we soften. The softening allows us to be human; it allows the difficulty to be held in a new way and connects us to all that we feel. This practice of 'turning toward' is about seeing if we can find a way within ourselves to hold the things that we find challenging; challenging about ourselves or challenging about what's going on in our lives, to allow them to live inside ourselves for a little while as if there's a safe and friendly place for them to be. Not trying to get rid of anything or fight with anything. It's about changing the inner environment just enough to welcome what is, to create the conditions that often allow things to resolve themselves, to heal, or to move in ways that allow new insights. If we criticize or try to fix or make them go away, we're not allowing some deeper, inner process to unfold or help heal.

I love author Toni Morrison's pragmatism about this kind of challenge.

I can be miserable if I want to. You don't need to try and make it go away. It shouldn't go away. It's just as sad as it ought to be, and I'm not going to hide from what's true just because it hurts.

There are times, though, when we have to say no to the things that arise. Maybe something is too painful, and maybe it's too soon to be processing a wounding experience. That's when we have to trust our sense of what an 'appropriate difficulty' is for us, and that will vary with each of us. Our nervous system can tell us when we are approaching too much; it can advise us to be cautious and suggest a different kind of allowing: that of allowing yourself to back off and directing your attention elsewhere, on a part of the body that is safe and feels okay, like hands, or by opening your eyes and looking around, or leaving the sit and going for a walk. This is bringing kindness to yourself, caring for yourself and learning that that, too, is possible in difficult moments.

Opening to our internal world can be hard work. But whether our life feels 'real,' whether we meet challenges with confidence, whether we hold ourselves and our life experiences with kindness - - all can be strengthened by how we meet our experiences sitting in meditation on retreat.

<u>Unconditional</u>

Willing to experience aloneness
I discover connection everywhere.
Turning to face my fear
I meet the warrior who lives within.
Opening to my loss,
I gain the embrace of the universe.
Surrendering into emptiness,
I find fullness without end.
Every condition I flee from,
pursues me.
Each condition I welcome, transforms me,
and becomes itself transformed
into its radiant, jewel-like essence.

Jennifer Welwood

27

However solid things may appear on the surface, everything in life is changing, without exception.
Sharon Salzberg

The Truth Of Change

The impermanence of things is conveyed instantly via the internet and news broadcasts. New information, the rapid pace of change; we are inundated with stories and events that underline the instability of "the way things are." It is our human tendency to turn away from what is unfamiliar, from the notion of change. Change is hard; doing things, thinking about things, how we approach the world - - we've established these habits over a lifetime, and we're reluctant to give them up. We can be stubborn about holding on to the familiar; we can be defensive about needing things to be a certain way.

Living with and through the pandemic challenged our human resistance to change, and we didn't have much choice in the matter. Human contact became unsafe. So did restaurants and grocery stores. CNN said that the office as we knew it was gone. Change happened, and it was beyond our control. Our views of what we took for granted as normal had been unceremoniously upended.

Yet - - here we are.

Surviving the pandemic required that each of us make adaptations in our lives; we've had to yield to the unexpected and find a way to cope with a shifting reality. We've had to create new ways to work, manage our families, and new ways to entertain ourselves without restaurants and, movie theaters and concerts. And in making these adaptations, we probably had to rethink some of our daily living habits and maybe some of our beliefs and assumptions. We had to overcome our innate resistance to change in order to craft our lives in these unprecedented conditions. And perhaps that necessity revealed qualities within each of us that we can savor.

Author Adam Grant writes about the value of rethinking, about adopting a kind of mental flexibility - - and about encouraging that same agility in others.

He goes so far as to say that taking on a stance of mental flexibility can begin to counteract what he called the "calcified ideologies that are tearing American culture apart."

He writes

It takes humility to reconsider our past commitments, doubt to question our present decisions, and curiosity to reimagine our future plans. What we can discover along the way can free us from the shackles of our familiar surroundings and our former selves. Rethinking liberates us to do more than update our knowledge and opinions - - its a tool for leading a more fulfilling life.

It sounds as if Grant is talking about what is needed to happen for each of us to navigate the recent pandemic. We had to rethink options and question what we do daily, whether about homeschooling the kids or figuring out how to get groceries. But the reason Grant's book caught my attention was that it suggests that fundamental principles of mindfulness are relevant to the notion of rethinking. For example, Grant maintains that we should treat our relationship to the ideas we hold as provisional - - that a given idea/belief that I hold at one particular time rests on what I know to be true at that time but may change if future evidence or facts cause me to question it. Certainly, mindfulness asks us to substitute curiosity for certainty. And reminds us that change is constant and nothing is permanent. Grant also claims that it's a sign of wisdom to avoid believing every thought that enters your mind and instead to become a witness to passing thoughts rather than becoming attached to them. Mindfulness similarly views thoughts as observable, ephemeral events: arising, appearing and then vanishing simply as movements of the mind.

This way of holding our ideas, beliefs and opinions more loosely also allows us to loosen the grip on our personal stories about who we are and what we are capable of doing. They make our boundaries a bit more porous - - not dissolved or unprotected - - but more open to other possibilities. Or, as Grant says, liberates us towards leading a more fulfilling life.

Meditation teacher Pema Chodron has a similar phrase for this more relaxed view. She terms it the flexibility of being. She says that a flexible identity is one that manifests as inquisitive, and adaptable, one with the capacity to relate without knowing, not figuring everything out, and not being at all sure of who we are or who anyone else is either. If we are too fixed in our identities - - beliefs, opinions - - "we have to busy ourselves with trying to rearrange reality because reality doesn't always conform to our view."

The practices of mindfulness and meditation allow us to bring awareness to our patterns and mental habits directly so that we become mindful of the thinking process itself. It is not about getting rid of thoughts. Thoughts are the source of all invention, creativity, and imagination not to mention problem-solving and educating. We need them to live our lives on a day-to-day basis. But without some awareness of how they influence us, we are at their mercy, and they do not always lead us in positive, wholesome directions. They can dominate our moods, limit our potential, and influence our experience.

The benefits of practicing meditation and mindfulness include not only revealing these thinking processes but also offering us a way to change our relationship to thoughts so that we are not so often carried away, not so often thinking negatively and not so often comfortable with the same old, same old…

And more often - - able to re-think, re-group, and survive pandemics.

<u>Yes</u>

It could happen any time, tornado,
earthquake, Armageddon. It could happen.
Or sunshine, love, salvation.
It could, you know. That's why we wake
and look out - - no guarantees
in this life.
But some bonuses, like morning,
like right now, like noon,
like evening.
William Stafford

Uncertainty

From the mindfulness perspective, uncertainty is a given. The nature of things - - all things - - is to change. Nothing stays the same. And this truth of life is often the source of anxiety and worry.

On a Tuesday in April, when I was 54 years old, I was diagnosed with uterine cancer. My doctor told me that he couldn't be specific about what was to follow until he and the consulting gynecological oncologist could feel my uterus, could hold the surrounding lymph nodes in their hands and, of course, until they had received the biopsy results from the organs they would remove from my belly. The outcome could range all the way from "You're cured - almost" to the ominously less specific "It has penetrated the wall of the uterus and spread."

The bottom line was that the extent to which the cancer had invaded my body wasn't to be known until I had surgery two weeks later - - two weeks until the prognosis and eventual aftermath were specified. That meant there would be two weeks of waiting, two weeks of total uncertainty about my future.

Fortunately, I had begun meditating some months before. My practice had already made me more aware of my physical sensations and had led me to tune into my body more often with more sensitive attention. Shortly after coming home with the diagnosis - - and with the word "pathology" and the sentence "You have cancer" in my head - - and after crying for several minutes,

I felt the surge of powerful emotions--from my belly up into my chest and throat. I made the choice then- and followed that choice through the next two weeks to meditate with these feelings. Whenever I began to feel overwhelmed by emotions during those two weeks, I would go to my cushion. I opened to that rush---and felt the fear, and felt the grief-- and sobbed. That cushion was in place full-time during this period. I didn't move it because I didn't know when I would need it. It itself became a refuge for me even though when I sat there, I was often crying or trembling. Since I had never experienced anything like this before, I didn't know what to do with these feelings but be with them. I didn't tell myself to keep a "stiff upper lip" or that I was being weak because I was 'giving in' to my emotions. I simply allowed myself to feel what I was feeling.

I became familiar with a new kind of fear. Though the thought of my own death had occurred to me before- after all, I was 54 - - it had always lived in my head as a rational, objective kind of knowing. Now, it was fully in my body as if every cell wondered if it would survive. It was remarkable to me, though, that the internal disturbance of these powerful feelings followed a pattern; if I stayed with the emotion, sort of riding it as a wave, it always crested, then subsided and ended in a letting go that brought a kind of peace. After going through this cycle a few times, I became both a witness and an actor in the process of release. It was neither a deliberate process- in the sense that I did not choose to be in it- nor a planful one- in that I didn't know nor could I control what would be happening next. I simply allowed myself to feel my painful regret….. and learned about self-forgiveness; I allowed myself to feel my constricting fear…. and learned that I could move through it to an openness for what was to follow. I also learned to trust this private practice as a means of relief; I could breathe and rest in it.

I sat often. It was exhausting. And it was amazing. The barriers that I usually constructed between myself and the world became apparent to me - - and they fell away. I was more clear about what I wanted- more decisive and able to state my preferences – than I had ever been before. And- at the same time- more able to be with what was happening inside me and around me.

I discovered so much during those two weeks that committed me to meditation and mindfulness for good. I learned that I could be with those very difficult emotions--that I was strong enough to allow that energy to be in my body without fighting or resisting. I discovered that that energy didn't last if given the time and space to course through. I learned that there was a peace, a calmness that followed the release of and yielding to what was already inside of me; that calm then allowed me to make clearer choices and be more present in the other aspects of my life that needed attention. I learned that acceptance wasn't about passively accepting the cancer and letting it run its course. I was going to have the surgery. I would take the necessary actions to restore my health. But it was about allowing the feelings that the diagnosis triggered to be experienced; it was about not pretending that I wasn't afraid; it was about giving myself the space to have a reaction, the space for the mind to settle so that I could see beyond the emotions that were so overwhelming. And I came to understand what I had heard so often before that facing a life-threatening event could be a gift.

A remarkable two weeks. But there is more to the story. Even though I had these healing, revealing, enriching experiences in meditation during this interval, they didn't last. Or continue to happen. Once I knew I would be OK, that the surgery had successfully removed the cancer and there was no trace of it elsewhere in my body, over the next few months, the sittings gradually returned to being ordinary. Nothing exceptional was happening anymore. I found that disappointing. But meditating had opened me to more of my inner life and to how my physical sensations were so closely linked to thoughts and feelings that I knew there was value to continuing the practice.

About two years later, I went on a weekend meditation retreat. I chose to schedule a private interview with one of the teachers because I wanted to ask about these shifts from extraordinary moments of practice to the now sometimes boring sittings.

When I met with the teacher and told him my story, the first thing he said was, "I know exactly what you mean. I have had cancer, too." And then he went on to say this.

Most of us live our lives on a horizontal timeline, with the past on the left and the future on the right. We spend our time mostly on one end or the other, with the present moment only a dot in the middle of the line. A catastrophic event- like the diagnosis of a life-threatening illness or 9/11 stops our motion backward or forwards on that line. As a result, our experience of the NOW expands. In that expansion, our hearts can open more fully. We live more intensely because we experience awareness so deeply. And compassion naturally pours out of the open heart. This arresting of motion is the place of coming home to ourselves, the place of meeting with that which some call the soul, some call our inherent Buddha nature. And it is the place of the unmanifest, the place of potential and possibility.

This teacher also told me that in that expansion of the present moment, I had glimpsed what it means to be awakened. To see with clarity, to act with wisdom, to be unencumbered by past conditioning.

Uncertainty is not going to go away. It is an 'unarguable'. How we relate to uncertainty - - accepting what we cannot change or arguing with what is already here - - is up to us.

<u>Ambiguity</u>

Learn to live with ambiguity,
with blurred lines, fuzzy edges,
fluid seams where one thing
spills into its opposite.

Be patient with all that is uncertain in your life.
Enjoy mixtures,
befriend apparent contradictions,
don't be in such a rush
to get closure every time.

Whoever said life was meant to be
one, pure, whole, and graspable?
And if by chance you spot
a little certainty fluttering nearby,
don't reach out for her

and clasp her madly to your chest
or hoist her high above your head
like some tiny tin trophy
or wield her like a club to force submission.

Instead, allow her to alight on the palm
of your open and trembling hand.
Rilke

A human being is a universe of experience, multifaceted and multidimensional. Each of us is a soul, a dynamic consciousness, a magical organ or experience and action. And each of us is in a constant state of transformation - - of one experience opening up to another, one action leading to another...This unfolding is constant, dynamic, and full of energy. This is the very nature of what we call life.
A.H. Almas

Flexibility Of Being

Our personal stories are an important/influential part of our personal identities. They can be hugely useful windows into the many ways to live this human life. They make us laugh. They remind us of our vulnerabilities. They reveal ordinary heroes and heroines. I heard one of those recently: a beautiful telling of a mother's persistence and brave advocacy in the face of her child's cancer diagnosis and treatment. This was the kind of story that lifts us and inspires us, that can make this life more livable and can help us remember the depth of kindness and compassion and courage within each of us. These are the stories that serve us, and often, they serve us whether we can pass the test of being true or not.

My story includes the fact that I am almost a first-generation American. All four of my grandparents, as well as my father, were foreign-born. It is a genetic fact that I am 100% Finnish. I grew up in a household in which both parents spoke Finnish, family gatherings were full of Finnish conversations, and whenever there was something my brother and I were not supposed to hear, my parents reverted to Finnish. When I was in high school, the foreignness of my family background sometimes embarrassed me and left me feeling different from my friends whose names were easy to spell and whose grandmothers could speak English. So, I didn't mention my Finnish-ness much, letting it stay somewhere in the background. My relationship with my heritage as an adolescent was tinged with that self-consciousness and was certainly ambivalent; one way with my family and another with my peer group. So I could imagine a scenario in which I had been rejected and bullied because of my last name or because Finland somehow created a disaster for this country and thus made Finns pariahs, or because someone in my family disgraced the Finnish name that I would then turn away from that heritage and try as hard as I could to become something other than Finnish. I would become attached to not being Finnish. Fortunately, none of those things happened. And my relationship with being Finnish had changed over time. As an adult, I have integrated the suomalainen into my being, especially after visiting Finland years ago and seeing my face and my maiden name and the names of my parents' friends wherever I looked.

This is one of the many changes that have occurred over time in the view I have of myself. My adolescent self is not the same as my senior adult self, and I'm sure almost everyone can recognize similar shifts in their self-view.

Yet, it is in our nature - - it is in the way our brains are structured - - to develop explanations, a narrative, to tie our experiences, our preferences and our beliefs together. We create our story. Otherwise, it's too confusing and too challenging for our need to feel in control, not to be able to make sense of our situation. Parts of these explanations will be factual and provable, like my Finnishness, but neuroscience is revealing that large portions will be fabrications. Our memories are notoriously inaccurate. We fill in the blanks, we distort, we forget. So our sense of who we are in this moment, the story of our identity, is not only one that we have created over time but is, more or often, less accurate.

From our Western frame of mind, the Self that is the star of our story is a stable, mostly unchanging version of the person we have always been. This version of the self keeps us on familiar ground - - and we really, really like the comfort of the familiar. But from the mindfulness perspective, this Self that is the star of our story is not the same self that we have always been, nor is it the same self that will be here tomorrow, even though we may try hard to keep it the same. (And in that trying hard lies much of the suffering that we encounter day to day!) Rather, this Self is a point, a particular dot in the process of unfolding that began the second we were conceived and will continue until we die. We are always in flux, according to this view, an ever-changing mix of ingredients that are influenced both by causes and conditions AS WELL AS -

- and here is the important part - - the nature of our intention regarding the NEXT moment that we step into. If we are conscious about our choices in the moment, if we are clear about what matters to us and what that requires of our hearts, minds and actions, then we can deliberately influence what unfolds in our futures. Obviously, we cannot change what has already happened to us, whether that has been mostly positive or mostly negative. Nevertheless, we can make a difference as to what will happen next in this life.

This way of holding our notions about the Self, about ourselves, opens the way to considering the future differently. For some of us, instead of believing that we are stuck in the groove of how we've always been, we can allow ourselves to imagine alternatives and take actions that lead in different directions.

Mindfulness practices help us loosen our grip on our stories and soften the edges of our egos. They make our boundaries a bit more porous, not dissolved or unprotected, but more open to other possibilities. Pema Chodron has a great phrase for this more relaxed self-view; she terms it the flexibility of being. A flexible identity is one that manifests as inquisitive and adaptable, one with the capacity to relate without knowing, not figuring everything out, not being at all sure of who we are - - or who anyone else is either. And by accepting and including more of ourselves, those parts we don't like, those habits that may be embarrassing, those thoughts we're not so proud of, we're allowing our vulnerability and accepting admission into the human race. We are also allowing for the possibility that we are far more than we believe ourselves to be. We are bigger than we know.

Trees And The Four Conditions

When my husband and I lived on several acres of land in the country, our house was situated on one end of a large meadow. Hundreds of feet away down the meadow, three trees paraded in a row behind one another, each somehow standing pretty much alone and not too close to the edge of the woods that bordered one side of the field. I often reflected on these trees because they were such great examples of how a tree of each particular type should look if all of the necessary conditions for thriving were in place. Sturdy, evenly branched, well-rooted, fully leafed out in the spring, balanced on all four sides. Each had enough space to spread as wide and reach as high as the true nature contained in its seed would allow. Each had enough rain to drink, enough nutrients in the soil to be nourished, and enough sun to flourish. Living healthy and long lives. They were really magnificent trees.

And I wondered. I wondered what I might have become had I experienced idyllic circumstances from the moment of conception. What would each of us be like, and what would the world be like if everyone were born from and into conditions that allowed for full flourishing in the way that these trees had flourished? I have to think that there would at least be much less suffering and probably much more joy. But in truth, none of us has had an ideally advantageous set of opportunities for developing.

When I first came across psychologist Paul Gilbert's description of the four conditions of being human, it resonated. He makes clear the categories of influences that can promote or interfere with our thriving in life. He claims that much of what determines our experience generally remains beneath the surface of our everyday awareness and has not been a matter of choice. Or, to use his phrasing is not our fault. But these are nevertheless influences within us that unconsciously can direct our thinking, feeling and behavior unless we become intentional about bringing them into our awareness; furthermore, every one of us is subject to these 'givens' that can lead us in both positive and negative directions.

Briefly, the four conditions of being human over which we have no control and that are not our fault are:

1. Our evolutionary heritage. Our brains and nervous systems have evolved to approach what is of benefit but also to protect us from threats. The latter is more powerful; as psychologist Rick Hanson reminds us, our brains are Velcro for the negative and Teflon for the positive. We remember and react more quickly to the dangers we face than to the pleasures we experience.

2. Our genetic composition determines so much of who we are, such as height, hand dominance, temperament whether we are better at math than English. Whether we have any musical ability or are tone-deaf.

3. Our conditioning from our families of origin and/or the households in which we were raised. We learned lessons early in life from parents, caregivers, siblings, teachers, etc., and we developed ways of coping with those lessons as best we could within the limitations of a child's or adolescent's capacities.

4. Social and cultural norms that vary by family, community region and country. A person raised in Tibet is exposed to very different values and ideas than a person raised in New York City.

Appreciating the degree to which these conditions have unknowingly (and often powerfully) carried weight in our lives can cushion the self-exploration that mindfulness and meditation require. It is not our fault. It is beyond our control, for example, that we have brains that continually generate thoughts, nor is it my fault that I have migraines. My mother passed those on to me. We can understand ourselves from a more sympathetic perspective and, perhaps, find a bit of softening toward some of our inherited peculiarities.

On the other hand, these conditions do not give us permission to continue patterns that are destructive to ourselves or to others. That they exist is one thing; that they do not have to continue to control our experiences is another. That there are skillful means for addressing problems these conditions have generated is yet another. Thus, Gilbert's caveat: These conditions may not be our fault, but what happens next is up to us. And that's where mindfulness and meditation can make a difference.

While none of us has had the perfect soil, nurturance and opportunities for flourishing as did the trees in the meadow, we do have the human gift of awareness that allows for choice.

Mindfulness and meditation cultivate that gift of choice.

The First Condition: Our Evolutionary Heritage

The first condition of being human, common to all of us, has to do with having that old brain. Poet Carl Sandburg described it this way:

A wolf in me...fangs pointed for tearing gashes...a red tongue for raw meat...and the hot lapping of blood. I keep this wolf because the wilderness gave it to me, and the wilderness will not let it go. not let it go.

This inheritance within each of us has important functions and manifestations. It keeps our survival energies alive, those instincts and motivations that scan for danger, that help us find food, that protect us. It houses anger, lust, anxiety, and - - surprise! - - joy. It is the home of our fight, flight or freeze response; it reacts quickly and automatically to perceived threats, whether to the proverbial snake in the grass or to the sticks that I often mistake for a snake.

For most of us, we are not faced with the dangers on a daily basis that our ancestors may have been. But the old brain doesn't always recognize that. It is not subtle. I think it is a great gift of neurological research that it has offered us a way to understand our baser impulses, our tendencies to withdraw or attack; it gives us the space to be gentler with ourselves as we navigate an increasingly complex world - - or the normal strains of relationships. And in offering us this allowance, it also opens the door to understanding others as members of the same species. If this is how I am, so is it how others are.

With respect to mindfulness and meditation, besides helping us understand our reactivity, a relevant finding from brain research is that we are, as Rick Hanson has said, velcro for the negative and teflon for the positive. Studies have demonstrated that it takes 5 times as many positive experiences to counteract a negative one. Apparently, the brain circuitry for threats is faster, registers more quickly and dominates the circuitry that processes pleasant experiences. The implications of this for mindfulness practices, for example, suggest that we should spend time savoring the positive in order to strengthen those neural pathways. Since I have never had a positive experience with a snake my aversion to them remains the same.

Nevertheless, the relatively recent research on our human brains suggests that there is a means for overcoming such instinctive reactions. The phenomenon of neuroplasticity offers the possibility that, with sufficient exposure, my reactivity to snakes could be reduced. Olga Klimecki, a researcher at the Max Plank Institute for Human Cognition and Brain Sciences, has studied a more important implication of neuroplasticity. Her studies have found that participants who received compassion training increased their ability to cope with stressful situations and suggests that the training "brought about fundamental changes in the ways the (subjects) processed distressing scenes."

Studies of the brains of dedicated meditators have provided evidence that, in fact, significant changes in the brain occur with consistent practice. For example, neural pathways that light up when kindness is the object of meditation can be strengthened over time. Both kinds of findings point to the increasing evidence of the brain's neuroplasticity.

Another evolutionary development that is important to our human functioning is the phenomenon of consciousness: our unique human ability to know that we know, to know that we think, to become aware of our own processing. This capacity for awareness is the basis for the important practice in mindfulness that calls for finding space before taking action in many situations.

These two elements of our human brain - - the primitive, protective aspects and the newer ability to become self-aware and intentionally choose our behaviors - - co-exist. Meditation and mindfulness practices offer us the opportunity to shift the balance from being totally under the influence of our protective instincts towards more measured, considered responses to our circumstances.

We are the culmination of 13 billion years of evolution. It has taken the universe these billions of years to grow organisms on the Earth that have a sufficiently developed consciousness to be able to reflect on and appreciate the simple fact of being here and to be able to look out consciously at the universe in wonder and awe...
Walter Truet Anderson

43

The Second Condition: Our Genetic Heritage

The second condition of being human, over which we have no control, has to do with our genetic composition. The characteristics and qualities in the genes that we inherit from our parents and our ancestors, interacting with our primitive brain structure, make us the unique beings each of us is at birth. As with any siblings except identical multiples, the arrangement of genes that arrived in me at conception differs from the arrangement that my brother received. Among other variants, he looks more like my mother and her side of the family; I resemble my dad and his mother. And I can thank my mom for migraine headaches, while my brother had my Dad to thank for his hay fever.

My lineage and genetic pool is 100% Finnish. All of my grandparents were born there, as was my father. But it was still surprising to me, when traveling in Finland, that I felt so at home, even though I could not speak Finnish and I visited no living relatives there. Partly, I felt at home because I saw my face and my father's face in so many places. And driving through the countryside seemed familiar because so much of it resembled the landscape in the upper peninsula of Michigan where all of my grandparents had settled as immigrants and which I knew from many visits there.

I was even more surprised by my experience when visiting the resting place of my great-grandparents in Halsua, Finland. Halsua is not even a town, really. The tiniest dot on a map with a commercial area consisting mainly of a corner store/post office/restaurant. When I asked a clerk in the store if anyone spoke English, she nodded that she understood me and then phoned the local school teacher to come by. I had only wanted to speak my mother's maiden name to people - - this was the place where her grandparents had lived - - but when the teacher arrived and heard my maiden name and that I was looking for my ancestors, she directed me to the church just down the road. There, she said, the young woman who was serving as an intern for the summer would be available to show me around the graveyard and her English was said to be good.

Besides this corner store, then, Halsua did have another major building: the Lutheran Church. Set in the woods amid towering evergreens rising at least 50 feet in the air, the clapboard building was modest in size and plain-faced in appearance. Behind and to the side of the church lay the most beautiful graveyard I had ever seen. Lovingly tended plots, highly polished markers, gentle pathways - - strangely inviting into the grounds sheltered by the fresh-smelling canopy high above.

As we approached the church, we were met by Hilde, the summer intern, who told us she knew all the family names on all the headstones. When I mentioned that both of my parents were Finnish, she asked for my maiden name. I wasn't expecting relatives from my father's side because his family had come from eastern Finland, and we were in the West, but when I told her I was a Heikkinen by birth, she laughed. The current pastor of the church had the same last name and, sadly, he and his wife had buried their first child in this graveyard not so very long ago; Hilde then guided us to the tombstone that carried the name I had had for the first 22 years of my life. After a quiet moment there, we were led to the graves of my great-grandparents, and Hilde returned to her work.

On this beautiful day, I sat on the ground in between the markers of my great-grandmother and great-grandfather. Tears came as I experienced a physical connection with this earth, with these foreign-sounding names, with my ancestors whose genes I now carry within me. I wasn't sad, at least not all sad, though I regretted that it had taken me so long to be there. My tears were more those of a child who had felt a little lost and now had seen the familiar faces of home - - the relief, the happy lifting of loneliness.

And in sitting by these graves, feeling an unexpected, atavistic homecoming throughout my body, I understood something about roots and about heritage and about belonging - - all on a physical level.

And then it came time to go. This lovely interlude was just for me.

We begin life with the world presenting itself to us as it is. Someone, our parents, teachers, analysts, hypnotizes us to "see" the world and construe it in the "right" way. These others label the world, attach names and give voices to the beings and events in it, so that thereafter, we cannot read the world in any other language or hear it saying other things to us. The task is to break the hypnotic spell, so that we become undeaf, unblind and multilingual, thereby letting the world speak to us in new voices and write all its possible meanings in the new book of our existence.

Sidney Jourard

The Third Condition: Our Family of Origin

I grew up in a family with a prevailing worldview of scarcity. My parents were children of immigrants, and each had experienced a lot of hardship in their childhoods as their non-English-speaking parents struggled to provide for their families. They often had to 'make do' just to 'get by.' And then my mom and dad lived through the Depression, so their sense of 'not much' was reduced to even less than that. It was not surprising then that money was always an issue in our household; never directly discussed but inferred. I learned early on, for example, that if I wanted anything, like the latest pair of shoes that all of my friends had, I had to solicit my mother secretly; then, if she funded the purchase, I was to hide the shoes from my father for a while. (In retrospect, I doubt that this strategy was effective in protecting my mother from having to explain the purchase, but neither was it an often used subterfuge.)

So this was the unconscious conditioning from my family that I brought into our marriage: that money wasn't to be discussed openly and that anything I might buy for myself was to be treated like contraband. And for several years, our conversations about money were terrible. First of all, I tried to avoid talking about finances in any way that I could. Philip, though, to his credit, was insistent that I knew where we stood financially, so from time to time, he would announce that we needed to have a conversation. (That was pretty brave of him, now that I think about it.) For a long time, my experience during these conversations was to shut down, tighten, and close myself off so that while physically there, I was not at all engaged. This was pretty evident to Philip and he naturally would find this irritating. Neither one of us was having a good time. So, eventually, once I started practicing mindfulness, I decided to approach this differently.

I began by informing Philip that I was going to try to handle these conversations more like a grown-up. I wanted him to know that I was making this effort. Then, when our discussion was about to start, I began paying attention to my physical experience. Boy, was I tight. My chest felt like it had a cement block sitting on it. The urge to get up and leave was powerful; if it was too strong, I would be asked for a moment so I could go to a place where I could breathe; if it was manageable, I would just breathe and release, breathe and release; once I felt some space in my chest and there was some room to listen, I signaled that we could continue. This became a practice. Our pattern was to have these conversations a few times a year, so I had many opportunities over time to be with this subject in a different way. Now, though not my favorite thing to do, I can sit and remain present and offer my opinion without the stress I once experienced.

Overcoming conditioning can take time. Something like this that was so strongly inside me physically: the tightness and contraction; mentally (I don't want to hear this; why do I have to do this; there is only bad news here) and emotionally (anger, why does he make me do this; fear - - oh, no, we won't have enough, etc.) And moving past a conditioning like this means that each of those parts has to be attended to.

How we relate to our conditioning matters. Whatever the resistance, the object of avoidance, the source of great tension, the issue that sparks unwarranted anger, whatever it is that is carried over into adulthood from childhood that constricts or narrows us, we can begin to meet it by shifting to an approach strategy rather than a resistant one. For me, it involved holding three attitudes toward my experience of aversion.

Forgiveness: not taking it personally! Understanding that the conditioning from my family was a major factor in my unskillful response to financial discussions helped me become willing to transform that response and gave me some space to not taking it so personally. I could offer myself some grace.

Curiosity and Interest: Opening to the experience of resistance itself. Allowing it and investigating it. Having practiced meditation and mindfulness, I had an understanding of how allowing the experience to be as it was and accepting the difficult sensations and unpleasant feelings could lead to releasing them. I had a trust that things could be different.

Kindness: Releasing self-judgment for how I had been handling the issue. Bringing kindness, in my case, meant including Philip, not doing this alone, and also meant not judging myself for the unskillfulness of my efforts. I also allowed myself to proceed at my pace. This process took place over time; it was definitely not a one-and-done. I had an aspiration but NOT a deadline!! If I had known then about the benefits of self-compassion, I would also have acknowledged how very painful this process was initially.

So the result of this for me is not only that I can now have these conversations. It also helps our relationship when I don't hide, avoid or look sour when it's time to talk. I discovered that I could STAND to be with this particular suffering, and in that sense, I was stronger than I thought. I have experienced a definitive fruit of these practices; I know that they can work - - so my commitment to continue practicing was reinforced. Because we could not control the prevailing influences that impacted us as we were growing up, every one of us is or has been under some kind of 'hypnotic spell' from our childhoods. We did not have the means when young to develop our own appropriate, skillful relationships with those influences that were harmful, deficient or unwise. The 'conditioning' I received around money and finances from my parents and the imprint it left on me as a child was not my fault. I formed beliefs on how to relate to money based on very little information and immature inferences. 'Breaking the hypnotic spell' of those beliefs took time, willingness and patience. But it could be done. The point is to be kind with ourselves, to bring an empathic awareness to those immature reactions. We can offer forbearance toward angry or fearful responses that seem extreme in the moment and understand that they may reflect the residue of attempts to protect ourselves when we were young. We can soften toward them so that we can release the contraction that accompanies them. In that sense, freeing them and ourselves. When we bring an empathic awareness to our unskillful defenses, we can begin to break the

> *hypnotic spell, so that we become undeaf, unblind and multilingual, thereby letting the world speak to us in new voices and write all its possible meanings in the new book of our existence.*
> Sidney Jourard

The Fourth Condition: Social and Cultural Norms

It's a VUCA world.

V- volatile, U-uncertain, C-complex- A- ambiguous. The acronym had been around for a while and was adopted by the military to describe the situation and conditions that soldiers in Afghanistan had faced. These are understandable adjectives to apply to a modern-day war zone. Then, the corporate world adopted these words to describe the business climate and the challenging experience of operating in an environment characterized by overwhelming amounts of information, global access, and a rapid pace of change. That's what VUCA has come to mean: the conditions that prevail in much of our contemporary world. The impingement of unsettling VUCA events on our lives seems relentless and has come to include school shootings, viruses, wars, and natural disasters.

And when external events are so jarring, we cannot help but be stirred internally - - making the process of coming to a quieter, more settled place for meditating that much more of a challenge. Two recent books have spoken to just this challenge: Bill Morgan's <u>The Meditator's Dilemma</u> and Nigel Wellings <u>Why Can't I Meditate</u>.

One of the authors sites the fact that meditation practices originated in cultures where the inward orientation of the contemplative traditions was honored; yogis or monks were, and are, seen every day on the streets, whereas the soup we swim in, our VUCA culture, does not support looking inward. Rather, our culture's mindset is outwardly oriented (70% extroverted), striving, self-doubting, and hurried, leading to our tendency to judge, evaluate, and believe that there is a right way to do things. These mental tendencies kick in right away when we sit. They kick in whenever we do anything 'wrong' or ineptly. They kick in when we compare ourselves to others.

Mindfulness teacher Tara Brach has pointed out that "meditation is a set-up for feeling deficient unless we respectfully acknowledge the strength of our conditioning to race away from Presence." Respectfully acknowledging and then offering ourselves some forgiveness, giving ourselves some space, for the cultural bias that we take into our meditation might ease the dilemma a bit.

And because meditation helps us understand and work with the human experience more skillfully, and because the human experience now includes the VUCA world, it would seem that the practices of meditation would be more helpful than ever.

Gil Fronsdal* (another teacher I like very much) talks about the three intangibles of Meditation. He named :

Silence

Space

Stillness

If we take a moment to reflect, we can see how these stand in contrast to Volatility, Uncertainty, Complexity and Ambiguity. Silence in contrast to the noise of all that information, all that disruptive noise of violence, all the noise of complexity; how space contrasts to the crowded field of complexity and multiple possibilities, to the chaos of volatility; how stillness contrasts with busyness, speed and the rapid pace of change. In a real sense, meditation can become a ritual of recovery - - for our brains, for our hearts, and for our bodies. Space, stillness, silence, each is a refuge that can offer relief, the opportunity to re-set, re-fresh, re-member, re-cover-, and reflect.

It is exciting to learn that neuroplasticity can help our brains evolve and change. But neuroplasticity works both ways. The more we react to VUCA unskillfully, the more prone we are to become stressed and the less able we will be to choose our response.

And as Thomas Merton has written:

To allow oneself to be carried away by a multitude of conflicting concerns, to surrender to too many demands, to commit oneself to too many good projects, to want to help everyone and everything is itself to succumb to the violence of our times.

*Gil Fronsdal: Guiding Teacher, Insight Meditation Center, Redwood, California AudioDharma.org

*Awareness is the primary currency of the human condition,
and as such it deserves to be spent carefully.*

Andrew Olendzki

Awareness

Just as suffering and change and uncertainty are realities of our human lives - - and just as it is a reality that we have had no control over the circumstances of our birth or our families of origin - - there is another reality of our human existence that can help us navigate these uninvited aspects of being human. And, importantly, it is a reality that can be cultivated to bring us greater wisdom and peace of mind. That reality is awareness.

On one of my first weekend retreats, Bhante Rahula, a Buddhist monk, delivered a dharma talk that kindled an important understanding of this gift of awareness. First, Bhante suggested the we imagine walking into an unlighted, dark room. He then asked us to imagine that soon after entering this unfamiliar space, we bump into an object. Moving further into the room, still unlighted, we continue to bump into one object after another. Eventually, we find a lamp and turn it on. We then begin to notice other objects, some hidden in the shadows; we find another lamp that illuminates more of the room, and we see the furnishing - - tables, chairs, sofa, and artwork. These things with shape, form, and volume immediately call our attention. But if we pause a bit and continue to look - - letting go of the thoughts that might have taken us into the room in the first place, letting go of any judgments we have about what we see - - we might notice whether the room seems stuffed with things or whether the room feels light and airy. With a bit more attention, we might become aware of the space that surrounds and holds the objects placed in it. Once we notice it, we can see that there is a lot of space around and over the contents of the room.

Similarly, when we sit in silence and put our attention on our minds, the contents may at first seem vague or clouded. In a while, though, we begin to see and can name the various objects in the space of our minds-objects like thoughts, feelings, memories, daydreams, and plans.

These objects or events can crowd the mind, seeming to leave little room for anything else; if we continue to pay attention, though, we notice that these objects come and go and change. As they come and go, we may glimpse that there is a space between the objects, just as there was an empty space between furnishings in the room. The space between the objects of the mind is a space empty of thought or feeling. Further reflection reveals that those activities of the mind occur in an open space, that is, the space of awareness. THIS AWARENESS IS ALWAYS THERE; we just don't normally pay attention to it because we're preoccupied with the objects, with the contents of our minds, just as when we walk into the furnished room and turn on the light, our attention goes to the tables and chairs, not to the empty space.

Not only is our attention highjacked by the objects of the mind, but we can then be seduced by them into digressions that lead us even further away from our present moment experience, digressions like planning future events or ruminating over past experiences. And this happens to all of us. The mind is constantly generating material for us to notice, and because of this activity, we come to believe that the mind equals, is the same as, the contents of the mind. But the mind is more than its contents; it is the space in which these contents are occurring, are arising and are passing away. We can take a figurative step back from seeing an object into the space of awareness;

Awareness is our uniquely human capacity to know that we are seeing those objects. We can not only have an experience, but we can know that we are having the experience as it is happening, and we can observe ourselves having the experience. This awareness is a powerful tool. As we sit in meditation, for example, we can develop awareness of our mind states, our heart states, of our body states. With practice, this information translates into our daily lives, allowing us to be more conscious of what we carry into our interactions with others, into our work life and into our relationship with ourselves. It can enable us to learn what brings us happiness and what leads to choices that bring pain. In a sense, awareness allows us to be awake to ourselves, to be awake in the world, to be awake to what enhances as well as to what undermines our well-being.

To be honest, though, I often need reminders to check in with myself. This is especially true- and especially helpful- when I am agitated, or when I am uncertain, or when I have been on one of those discursive-mind journeys. Asking myself "What am I aware of now?" It is using awareness to recognize what is present in me; it is intentionally creating space to allow what is there to be there without having to react; it is allowing me time to choose a response.

Only when we are aware can we seize opportunities for conscious choices and live according to what is important to us. That space of awareness allows us to step outside the contents of our mind, to see without pre-judgments, beyond what we already know, toward new possibilities. And when we do, we are freer to discern what matters at the moment.

In this sense, we might think of awareness as a holding environment, the place of safety and spaciousness where whatever is is met with caring and is allowed, the ultimate resting place. Awareness is always there behind whatever is seducing our attention at the moment. It has the capacity to free us, at least for each timeless moment that we step into it.

...the challenge is twofold: first, to bring awareness to our moments as best we can, in even little and fleeting ways. Second, to sustain our awareness and come to know it better and live inside its larger, never-diminished wholeness.
Jon Kabat-Zinn

Awareness-
her gaze is so constant,
our every move
watched
with such affection,
a ceaseless vigil
without condition
or agenda,
silent,
patient,
unrelenting in her
embrace.

There is endless room in
the heart of this lover,
infinite space for whatever
foolishness we may
toss her way.

But she is also
crafty, this one-
a thief who will steal away
everything we ever cherished,
all our beliefs,
all our ideas,
all our philosophies,
until nothing is left
but her shimmering
wakefulness,
this simple love
for what is.
                John Austin

There is a force within you that gives you life - -
Seek that
In your body lies a priceless jewel - -
Seek that
Oh, wandering Sufi
If you are in search pf the greatest treasures
Don't look outside
Look within, and seek That
                Rumi

FINDING OUT WHAT IS TRUE: Meditation

Two Questions

I attended my first mindfulness retreat, a weekend in the '90s, at Bhavana, a Buddhist monastery in West Virginia. The experience there, to the newby that I was then, seemed austere and somewhat strange. I slept in a kuti, a one-room cabin with no water, electricity, or heat; there were no meals after 11:00 am; men and women sat separately on different sides of the meditation hall; there were many rules about how to behave in the presence of the monks. My sketchy notes from that time revealed how uncomfortable I was, both physically and mentally. I was still new enough to meditation that sitting cross-legged on the floor for an hour was excruciating on my body, and, of course, my mind was anything but settled. I struggled.

On the other hand, the messages I heard that weekend were so uplifting and unbinding: messages like "you have the inner intelligence to guide yourself; there is room for doubt and questions; take these ideas as hypotheses to be tested by you; in this retreat, you probably will be uncomfortable; that's normal; your mind will do all kinds of things; of course it will; minds do that." During these few days, an unbinding from my own expectations of myself, from "shoulds," from what I thought was supposed to be happening had begun. It was as if what I was experiencing there was already known. In the unconventional environment at Bhavana, hearing these messages was reassuring. If these parts of my experience were already known and understood, maybe what else was said during the weekend about our abundant human capacities for kindness and compassion - - maybe was also true. The hook was cast and taken early.

Practicing meditation and mindfulness has indeed proven to me that investigating our internal world leads to a deeper understanding of ourselves and that that understanding, in turn, can lead to a more easeful, aware and compassionate way to live this life.

While it is hard to know whether my brain circuitry has actually changed (as research has claimed is possible), I can cite two significant benefits of my practices, both of which have stealthily become part of my being. I say stealthily because these practices can gradually chip away to lessen the reactions and beliefs that are not of benefit to us, as well as slowly cultivate and strengthen those attitudes and qualities that enrich our lives. It doesn't happen overnight, though.

An early meditation instruction suggested simply asking the question, "What's happening right now?" The meditator then directs awareness to sensations in the body, to the activity of the mind and to whatever feelings are present, beginning with what most calls his/her attention. This practice, over time, revealed to me a trifecta of thought, sensations and emotions that creates an " inner atmosphere" and that this inner atmosphere heavily influences how I end up being in the world. I came to understand the power of the connections among what thoughts I entertain, what happens in my body and what actions I take in my life. It has made all the difference to me to pay attention, whether I am meditating or walking in my neighborhood, sitting in a meeting or having a conversation with my husband and ask: what inner atmosphere is here? Or, as teacher Tara Brach phrases it, what is the weather inside? Just paying attention to the climate of my attitude has mattered immensely. And this then leads to further questions: am I open to this or not? What else is here? It often leads to the inquiry that deepens my understanding of what I am processing/experiencing at the moment; it's important because this is the point at which a shift can take place. The point at which a choice is possible.

This raises the second important mindfulness question: How do I want to be with what I am finding? How do I want to relate to what is happening? By asking this question while meditating brought more awareness to the nature of my inner dialogue and the effect of the words I was using in the dialogue. My inner voice was often harsh, critical, and negative; by recognizing how that impacted my body (tightness in the chest) and my felt state (discouraged), over time, my relationship with myself has changed. It has helped me reduce the frequency of those icky times when I say to myself, "Why in the world did you say that?" It gives me the opportunity to release what might be unskillful and to cultivate /nourish within what is skillful. I feel "mostly" forgiven; I am gentler and less judgmental of myself - - which naturally translates into being gentler and less judgmental in other relationships. This practice also enabled a shift toward being more in alignment with what matters to me and more in alignment with how I want to be with others. And more in harmony with myself.

There is, furthermore an 'outlook' or view behind these practices that keeps me meditating. For one thing, they are founded on a compassionate view of our human condition. It's a relief that the first thing Jon Kabat-Zinn tells a new Mindfulness-Based Stress Reduction (MBSR) class is that there is "more right with you than wrong with you." The focus of the class then becomes about what gets in the way of that inherent rightness so that we can then shift our way of relating to our lives, and meditation and mindfulness give us means for shifting that relationship.

It's such a hard concept, though: that there's nothing wrong with us, that whatever is here in this moment, the good, the bad, or the ugly, is not a statement about our inherent goodness or badness, that we can stop struggling to make ourselves something other than we are. At least it has been for me. But I realized as I've looked through notes that I've taken over the years that I have discovered my optimism through these practices. Because it is optimistic, isn't it - - this foundational belief that we already have everything we need to become more awake and more aware. More the whole of who we are.

I love this quote from Wayne Muller. For me, it captures both the quality of an inner voice speaking from this wholeness as well as the sense of promise that manifesting this quality holds.

> *What if we actually believed that this hidden wholeness was really true? What if, as an experiment, if only for one day, we lived as if we believed that there lived in us some reliable strength, wisdom, and wholeness? What if we were to pretend that, regardless of our health or mood, our fortunes or circumstances, we would remain quietly wise, accurate, and trustworthy in our judgments and actions? Even more, what if we could actually feel, sense, and know, with unshakable certainty, that wherever we went, into whatever company or situation we were called, we would carry with us always this capacity to move with confidence and trust into any situation? How would we think, act, choose? How would we respond differently to the world during such a day?*

Beginning Meditation

When I first began meditating, I was totally embarrassed - - humbled, really - - by what was revealed to me as I sat and witnessed myself. Sometimes for what seemed to be the entire 20 minutes, which was all I could do at the beginning, the most recurrent thought was about my hair; I didn't like the cut, should I let it grow, etc., etc. I WANTED to be deeper and more profound, but no - - there it was again: " Maybe I should try a different stylist." I then began calling myself names like superficial, trivial and shallow. In other words, I was judging my experiences, and as I did so, I became caught in negativity, my body tightened, and I couldn't wait for the 20 minutes to be over. It was not a pleasant experience. And I've learned that is often the case in meditation. What is revealed to us in this process of paying close attention can be humbling, sometimes painful and often uncomfortable. This can be a turning point in a practice. The question becomes one of whether we are willing to stay with whatever arises, unpleasant or pleasant, and not turn away from the experience because we don't want it to be that way. Fully accepting what is rather than struggling to change it allows the internal weather to be as it is, not denying that there is unpleasantness, not trying to make a rainy day sunny. As the poet Rumi writes:

<u>The Guest House</u>

This being human is a guest house.
Every morning a new arrival.

A joy, a depression, a meanness,
some momentary awareness comes
as an unexpected visitor.

Welcome and entertain them all!
Even if they're a crowd of sorrows,
who violently sweep your house
empty of its furniture.

Still treat each guest honorably.
He may be clearing you out
for some new delight.

The dark thought, the shame, the malice
meet them at the door laughing,
and invite them in.

Be grateful for whoever comes
because each has been sent
as a guide from beyond.

I had to learn to practice acceptance, to treat honorably my irritation and to 'welcome' the arrival of thoughts that were not what I wanted them to be. With the help of a teacher and with further practice, I began to take a look at the nature of the relationship I had with my internal experiences. I began to practice holding this stream of internal events with more spaciousness or more gentle acceptance, without judgment. To being "grateful for whoever comes." What I had been seeing in my "hair thoughts" and experiencing in my irritation was my "humanness," my ego self, my personal concerns taking over, clouding the sky of awareness, drawing me into a smaller and smaller way of being. But I learned that rather than condemning myself and going into a cycle of self-blame and negative self-talk, I could CHOOSE to offer myself some kindness, some softness instead. And I could arrive at the place where my thoughts were just thoughts and not comments on my worthiness or my abilities as a meditator or as a person.

In time, I found myself witnessing this thought parade instead of marching in it. Eckhart Tolle calls this "Space Consciousness" and describes it as an "alert inner stillness in the background while things happen in the foreground;" he also says that this dimension is there in everyone when we discover that stillness, we can return to the space of awareness instead of being caught by the distractions in the foreground.

With every small 'allowing' or gentle welcome, more space is created around our experience. That is the space that can move us from reactivity to wise responding. It is the room in which the heart's aspiration can arise and become manifest. It was Victor Frankel, a holocaust survivor, who famously said, "The space between the S, the Stimulus, and the R, the Response, is the space of freedom." If we can inhabit that space, we become more open to receiving the present moment just as it is - - without coloring it with our fixed ideas or our typical emotional reactions. Once we have this clear awareness, our habitual tendencies, mentally, emotionally and physically, can become unhooked from the chain of events, and we have the freedom to respond deliberately, intentionally and more skillfully to our subjective experiences instead of reacting automatically based on conditioning or instinct.

So mindfulness is not about the 'why' but about the 'what is;' it's not about the past or the future but about the present. And it is about connecting, in that space between the S and the R, with intention. How do we most want to be? To what do we incline our hearts, minds and bodies? Then, by being able to act to be true to those intentions, we can live more in that place of the sacred pause and from that place of mindfulness.

As John Kabat-Zinn has written:

The very act of stopping, of nurturing moments of non-doing, of simply watching, puts you on a different footing with your future. How? It is only by being in this moment that any future moment might be one of greater understanding, clarity, and kindness, one less dominated by fear or hurt and more by dignity and acceptance. Only what happens now happens later.

An Act Of Love

It is 6:30 am, and a bell rings three times to signal the end of my morning meditation. As I open my eyes, I notice that the darkness of the room is touched by the faint light of the day's beginning. I notice, too, that I am reluctant to move. I love sitting in the early morning when the quiet of the house and the quiet of the world seem to support the settling of my mind.

And today's sit was an especially gentle one.

I feel gratitude that I can begin my day with this inner quiet. I say thank you for this gift. With that, I stir myself into movement. I glance at my iPad - - the app that rang the bell also shows where on the globe other meditators are practicing, an ironic juxtaposition of 21st-century technology tracking a 2500-year-old practice. I see dots In Australia, Spain and Southeast Asia. And, if those dots are looking at their devices, they see a dot in Richmond, Virginia, USA. We are a global sangha/community.

While every religious and spiritual tradition includes forms of contemplative practice, I have chosen Vipassana or insight meditation, the same practice that brought enlightenment to the Buddha. A key component of this practice is mindfulness: directing attention to one's experience as it is happening without judgment. While meditating, this mindful attention is placed on one's subjective experience of sensations, thoughts and emotions. Over time, the practitioner develops an intimate awareness of her inner life: the pleasant, the unpleasant and, as they say, the good, the bad and the ugly. And with that awareness comes a clearer understanding of how our inner life affects how we are in the world.

The interest in meditation and contemplative practices has mushroomed over the last 30+ years. Research into the benefits of mindfulness meditation is especially compelling; it has a demonstrated impact on lowering blood pressure and strengthening the immune system; in schools, it has led to improved attention spans and increased resilience; the general population reports greater well-being when using these techniques. But as I reflect on my practice - - why

I choose to continue the practice, to study about it and to teach it - - I find it has as much to do with my mother, my husband and my grandchildren as it does with me.

I meditated for my mother because this practice has taught me about my impatience. My mother lived to be 100 and suffered from several of the infirmities that are expected at such an advanced age. For several years, being with her required an adjustment in my sense of time. Everything took longer, whether moving from place to place or simply ordering a meal. Practicing mindfulness of the body, I had come to recognize the early physical signs of impatience, the tightening of the jaw and ears, and to use these cues as reminders of my intention when I was with my mom: the intention that my actions arise from a place of love rather than impatience.

I meditate for my husband, well, really, for our marriage. One of the principles of this practice is that by turning toward rather than avoiding the difficult, we can move through disturbing or unsettling situations instead of avoiding or leaving the issue unresolved. With my spouse, I have learned to pause in tough conversations, step back and breathe, ask for a 'moment,' and consider what I need or want to say. He benefits by having to guess less often about what I am thinking, and I am more effective in speaking my voice in the relationship.

And I meditate for my grandchildren. I recognize now that for so much of my son's earlier years, I was too busy with my own striving in graduate school and career to be fully present to him. Now, as a grandmother, I want to be more intentional. When I am with my grandkids, I want to be with them - - not somewhere else in my mind. My practice has helped me come back to the moment, to stay in the moment with them, to cherish the moments.

I am far from perfect in any of these areas: impatience, being with the difficult or being present. I miss the mark a lot. But my being and doing are more often aligned with my intentions than they used to be. And I attribute the increased richness of my life to these early morning sits, to silent meditation retreats and to simple acts of mindful presence that have unexpectedly turned out to be 'gestures of the heart.

The most difficult of all possible tasks is to come to understand one's own mind.
        Joseph Goldstein

Why Meditate

Much of the emphasis on mindfulness in the media caters to our hurry-up culture by focusing on brief practices that can bring us more into the moment as we go through our day. These on-the-spot practices are helpful in slowing us down a bit and in making mindfulness more accessible to those who may be daunted by the thought of silence and sitting still.

But it's important to be reminded how formal meditation practices fit with mindfulness and to understand why they are worth the investment of our time.

Joseph Goldstein, a pioneer in bringing meditation and mindfulness to the United States, is a resource for helping us understand how meditation deepens our mindfulness and impacts our lives. He says that meditation does three things:

Opens what is closed.

Balances what is reactive.

Reveals what is hidden.

1. <u>Opening what is closed:</u> If we just consider the importance of the body in mindfulness meditation, we can touch into some of what Goldstein means by this. For many of us, and for this Western culture in general, we ignore the body in favor of the mind. We do not take into account the information that the body has to offer us about our well-being, about how we respond to stress, and about how to recognize signs of illness. Practices that reconnect us to our bodies, beginning with simple breath practice, can help us cultivate awareness of those signals and can open us to a physical knowing of ourselves that also offers a deeper connection with our human condition. In fact, the same can be said for any of the

meditation practices; the heart practices of kindness and compassion, in particular, can open us to our true natures as worthy beings. Opening what is closed in general means that we become more whole and more able to include all of who we are as we go about our lives.

2. <u>Balancing what is reactive:</u> One of the hallmarks of mindfulness programs, Mindfulness-Based Stress Reduction (MBSR) most notably, is the emphasis on changing our relationship to our experience of difficult emotions, thoughts, sensations and situations. Every one of us is naturally triggered by certain stimuli that, for reasons of past conditioning in our families combined with our brain structure, are associated with fear or threats to our well-being. We react out of our need to protect ourselves. It is a part of how we have evolved out of necessity as human beings. But for the most part, those threats and our fears are unfounded IN THE PRESENT MOMENT; in other words, the immediate situation is not dangerous but somehow shares elements of the past and so provokes our reaction.

Meditation helps us balance that reactivity. Take a simple example from the body. While meditating, we may notice that our left knee hurts; there is a sharp, stabbing sensation. We react by wanting that sensation to stop and either move our knee to a different position or shift our focus to another body part. But mindfulness asks us to deal with this experience differently. It invites us to STAY with the sensation if we can, for a few seconds if that's all that's possible, and thereby begin to recognize that we have the capacity to turn toward the difficult, to handle discomfort in a different way. The same kind of attitude, that of a willingness to be with what is unpleasant, is also applied in meditations that focus on difficult emotions such as anger or sadness. (Just for this breath, can I be with this pain?) As we practice this 'staying' in meditation, we build the muscle of resilience, of the capacity to turn toward those life events that are challenging. We balance our reactive tendency, that urge to avoid the difficult, to 'not see' or to cover over our problems. We balance it with the strength to deal with what is happening as it happens, with what life presents to us so that we can move through such challenges. Balancing what is reactive.

3.   <u>Revealing what is hidden:</u> This revealing happens on at least two levels, probably on many more levels in meditators more experienced than I am. We all experience one level of revealing almost immediately when we begin to meditate. This is the discovery of how very busy our minds are. We don't normally pay attention to the cacophony that is occurring almost all the time. On that same level, the more we meditate, the more we discover how we speak to ourselves; we discover patterns in our thinking; we begin to recognize the relationship between what we think and how we feel in an intimate way; all of these revealed as we sit with mindful attention to our subjective experience.

And, there is more.

We notice the transience of our subjective experience. A thought doesn't last. The energy of an emotion arises and passes. We become familiar with the truth of impermanence at a cellular level. And as we do, we begin to notice in our lives what that might mean for how we choose to live. When we embrace a practice of compassion or kindness, we not only discover within ourselves more and more of our true nature but we understand in an embodied way that we are connected to every other being in our vulnerability, in our common humanity. Our belonging is revealed, and our core goodness is seen.

For more, see Joseph Goldstein's <u>Insight Meditation: The Practice of Freedom</u>, Shambala, 1994.

Presence

"Live as if Everything is Important." This is the title of a dharma talk by meditation teacher Gil Fronsdal. (He is the co-founder of the Insight Meditation Community (IMC) in Redwood, California; his talks are posted on the web at AudioDharma.) In this talk, he tells a story about being on a seven-day Zen retreat. Apparently, there are strict rules about how to behave in a zendo; most movements and transitions are choreographed, including the daily offering of tea. At the beginning of this particular retreat, each person was given a tea cup to use for every afternoon tea service; the cup was to be returned ceremonially on the last day. Fronsdal happened to be seated next to a Zen monk for those seven days; he reports taking careful note of his companion's dignified stillness and being inspired by the equanimity emanating from him. But the monk, at the end of the retreat, surprised Fronsdal by disturbing the ritual of returning the tea cups. When the tray with the other tea cups was presented to him, instead of formally placing his cup on it- as everyone else had done - - the monk first bowed deeply to his cup.

Fronsdal goes on to say that this may seem silly on the hearing of it - - paying that kind of attention to a tea cup - - such a small detail of life to receive that significant a focus. But as he reflected on this over time, he realized that that act had been an expression of the monk's mind state - - a mind state that saw and then treated even a teacup as if it was important. Bowing to the cup displayed his gratitude for how it had served him and for what it contained.

This lesson became folded into Fronsdal's personal practice. He began holding the intention to go through his day with enough presence of mind to see that everything was important. And he reports finding that, to the extent he does that - - he gives his full attention to what is right there in front of him, whether to the chair he's sitting in, to the person walking down the street, to the orange he is eating - - that his world has become more sparkling, more rich, more alive.

He acknowledges that that way of being might seem impossible to you or to me. But, if it is our view that some things are not important, that whatever is here is not as important as the plans for whatever is next, that what is here now is not as worth my time as what is in my imaginings - - if that's how things are seen - - then that is true. What is here becomes unimportant, and that's how you will come to see your life.

But if instead, we see everything as a part of the fullness of life - - when, in Fronsdal's words, "everything we encounter becomes part of our deeper conversation with reality or the conversation that reality is having with us" - - then that is what's true. It's true, Fronsdal says, because importance lives in our mind, in our view, in our understanding. He asks: Is everything important? If yes or no, it's a self-fulfilling prophecy. It's one of those things that becomes true because you see it that way. And, there is no absolute about this. It's your choice, he says, about what kind of world you live in - - one where you actually see and touch and experience what's here or one in which you are living in another dimension of time. Living now, in the present moment, or dwelling in the past or the future.

Bringing this teaching into my personal experience: do I expect to be able to live as if everything is important? No- I really don't. I don't have the steadiness of attention to stay present in every moment and every aspect of my experience. Nor do I always have the clarity of 'seeing' that is necessary to appreciate the importance of all that is contained in a given situation. Too many judgments, preferences, or reactions may be coloring or clouding my view at that moment. But what Fronsdal does for me is to call the question: On what do I CHOOSE to spend my time and attention? In what dimension - - the now, or the then, or the not yet - - do I choose to live?

And I know this. I have experienced moments when those clouds have not obscured my vision when I could clearly see, take in and be present in the experience of something as it was happening, and those moments have been more vivid, integral, unconditional, and heartfelt.

One of those moments occurred on a retreat when I was leading a meditation in front of the room; this was toward the end of the weekend, so the silence during meditations deepened with time. To experience the visual of all of us sharing this silent space, I intentionally opened my eyes; in attempting to describe what then happened within me and to me during those few moments, I can't capture in words the completeness of it. The best I can do now: as I gazed at the gathering of meditators, I could simultaneously see and feel the power of that mutually held silence; it was palpable. I was deeply moved by so many of us practicing so sincerely together; my heart felt the human vulnerability of all of us; there was just a wordless connection in that field of energy. And that doesn't begin to convey it. It wasn't until later, when reflecting on this experience that I recognized that in those moments, there had been nothing between me and that experience, no thoughts, no stories, no expectations. Just what was. And, along with all the other meditators, I was a part of "the ocean of being."

I think that's what Fronsdal was talking about. That's what presence is. It is fully experiencing; in a sense, it is being experienced. So, if it sounds hokey, well, hokey is pretty amazing.

And another thing I do know: I wouldn't have had that moment if I didn't have my practice. If I didn't, like Fronsdal, at least have the intention to become more awake to the experiences of life. If I didn't believe that practices to become more awake were important enough to spend my time on them.

Eyesight
It was May before my
attention came
to spring and

my word I said
to the southern slopes
I've

missed it, it
came and went before
I got right to see:

don't worry, said the mountain,
try the later northern slopes
or if

you can climb, climb
into spring: but
said the mountain

it's not that way
with all things, some
that go are gone
                Archie Randolph Ammons

Meditation As Antidote

Mindfulness meditations rest on the basic assumption that we all have the capacity to live in an open and free way, a way that allows us to be with the more difficult realities of life like illness, aging and eventually, dying - - yet also equally with the joys and well-being that are the blessings of life. Or, in Joseph Campbell's familiar words, with the 10,000 joys and 10,000 sorrows that living in this human body inevitably brings.

But it is also inevitable, because of the way we humans are made, the way our brains are wired, that beginning in early childhood, as we develop our sense of who we are, we not only begin to create strategies to get more of what we want (the pleasant stuff) and less of what we don't want (the unpleasant) but we also sense that we sometimes need to protect ourselves from the threats to our well-being that our surroundings present. Whether those threats are psychological or physical in one sense doesn't matter; we, when young with limited resources, develop ways to guard ourselves from hurt and pain and to soothe ourselves when injured or deprived. It is those strategies we form early on for self-care and self-enhancement that can later interfere with the more fundamental capacities to live openly, freely, and fully as ourselves.

Mindfulness meditations are both the antidotes to and the means for releasing ourselves from those self-gratifying and/or protective habits that no longer serve us and may, in fact, get in the way of living life with greater authenticity and happiness. For example, if our strategies became about avoiding pain, mindfulness meditation asks us to turn toward that which is difficult and learn, by staying with it, that we are stronger than we thought. If our strategies are about blaming and turning anger on others because of real or perceived harm, meditation takes us into the energy of that anger beneath the story in which it is woven to transform it into compassionate action, most likely for ourselves. If we learn to please others to gain approval, attention or love, meditation can shine the light on our inherent 'enoughness' to enable establishing boundaries in our relationships that include our own needs and dignity...

Of course, none of these possibilities happens immediately. It has taken time and years to establish the ways in which we have preserved our sense of ourselves and what we need to do to live as we do. So it will take time to undo, replace or release those ways. And it begins with training the mind to settle enough so that we can see what is getting in our way.

And that training happens through meditation.

Intimate Meditation

I have discovered that Vipassana meditation is a most intimate practice. There is no one to impress, no one to resist, no one from whom to withhold your truth. There is only me. And if I choose to hide, I will have to hide from myself. If I choose to deceive, deny, or pretend, I am choosing to take those actions against myself. And as Tara Brach has stated, "What you are willing to experience is the boundary to your freedom." So, if I elect not to stand next to the fires of my inner being, my judgmental thoughts, my pettiness, my resentments, and my disappointments, I am only limiting the extent to which I can experience my life.

Welcome To Whoever You Are

You know how sometimes you read a sentence that says something you already know but it suddenly strikes you so differently that you see a familiar thing in a completely different way? Well, that happened to me a while ago. The sentence was about the simple fact that each of us breathes differently; that some of us breathe 12 times a minute and others of us breathe as many as 15-20 times a minute, and that however many breaths we take in any given normal minute are natural to us. What is the same is that we all breathe; what is different is that there is no one way to breathe.

Why did this strike me so much? I had been thinking a lot about shoulds and oughts and how, even in the practice of meditation, many of us think there is a way to do this and that we're not getting it right. And that also seems much more generally true - - that somehow there is a way to DO life - - and that many of us seem to think that we're not getting that right either.

When we spend time in quiet reflection or meditation, it is a given that we will be visited many times by thoughts, feelings and sensations that are uncomfortable, unpleasant or unwanted. Whether it's simply sleepiness or whether it's regrets, worry, or even intense grief, whether it's an old set of judgments or a familiar story, this phrase, work on becoming a native of mind, a native of heart, suggests that we view these internal experiences as natural, that they occur because we are made the way we are made. Similarly, an important part of mindfulness meditation is cultivating the skill to see these arisings as 'native' phenomena, as the natural outputs of our minds and physiology. When we can do that, we become able to view these experiences less personally; we learn not to identify with or become lost in thought trains or emotionally tinged stories. And we begin to be able to let go of shoulds and should-nots, like 'I shouldn't be tired, or I shouldn't feel that way.' We learn to soften negative judgments such as 'it's wrong of me to think about that' or 'I'm a bad person for feeling that.'

I remember when I was a teenager being very aware that my friends and their families lived differently from mine. Most were from more affluent circumstances than I was, and I thought that there were rules, social rules, that they knew and I didn't. That sense of being on the outside, of feeling as if I was either a step behind or on the verge of making a mistake, often left me looking outside of myself for the right things to say and even to feel. For a long time, I had the sense that I would embarrass myself or blow it somehow.

As it turns out, I eventually learned that a faux pas was not such a terrible thing, nor did violating some rule of social conduct necessarily mark me as an outcast. It has been a learning curve over the years to the freedom of discovering my own belonging; instead of searching outside of myself for what works, what fits, and what matters, I can consult and trust my inner knowing for guidance. That's what the line from the poem: "Work on becoming a native of mind, a native of heart," suggests to me. And, in a way, that echoes one of the teachings that early on welcomed me into meditation practice. Just as I heard that there were many ways to breathe, so it was when I heard the instruction that we were to rely on our own experience to tell us whether the meditation practices were of benefit and that their value depended on our personal sense of their merit. This offered me choice and agency. I felt both a permission and a relief.

There is also underneath these practices the foundational belief that we already have everything we need to become more awake and more aware. More the whole of who we are. It is here now within us. We are enough. That native mind and that native heart are enough. These practices are about discovering that native mind and that native heart.

Discovering my natural rhythm of breath, my natural rhythm of walking. Accepting without resistance the natural flow of my internal experience; noticing without attaching or rejecting whatever is happening within the life stream at the moment. These practices offer me the room to customize, to learn what works best for me, whether the anchor of the breath or whether I settle more quickly with sound; whether I sit in a chair or on the floor, whether I open to my senses on a given day or choose to do a heart practice.

It's such a hard concept, isn't it - - that there's nothing wrong with us; that whatever is here in this moment, the good, the bad, or the ugly, is not a statement about our inherent goodness or badness. We can simply stop struggling to make ourselves something other than we are. At least it was for me. Thankfully, meditation helps us chip away at the conceptual barriers of shoulds and oughts. And we can then more readily align ourselves with the life within us - - our heartbeat, our flow of energy, the sensations of vitality - - bringing us more into harmony with the life around us.

What And Why

Years ago, Philip and I were planning to lead a silent meditation retreat at our house. I remember telling my mother about it, that 20 people would come and spend the day together, mostly in silence. Her response was, "All day in silence?" I said, "Well, from 10:00 to 3:30 - - most of the day." And she said, "I can't imagine 20 people in your house all day not speaking to each other!" When it was put like that, it did sound kind of odd.

It seemed reasonable not only for my mother to have asked but for us to ask ourselves as well: What is this odd thing that we do, and why are we doing it? A simple answer may be that we are following an urge or a pull to become more internally spacious and quiet and perhaps to open our hearts more fully. The energy pressing these urges often comes from feeling just the opposite - - rushed, tight, and wanting some relief. And we wouldn't be doing these practices if we didn't have some belief that meditation and mindfulness will help us find that relief.

In fact, a basic premise of vipassana or insight meditation, is that each of us has within us a core that is caring, calm and contented, a natural presence that is both wise and compassionate. The problem is that our history of conditioning, as well as our attempts to manage the natural energies of our bodies and the unending proliferation of thoughts that the mind generates, all combine to create obstacles that interfere with and obscure that natural presence. Meditation is a practice that allows us to become more aware of what is between us and that presence and that peace.

This came home to me, not for the first or last time, several years ago when I attended a conference with my husband. The conference was geared toward professionals who were mostly business types, and though I had some interest in a few of the sessions, this was an unfamiliar crowd of people. It did not take long for me to feel out of place and pretty disconnected from my surroundings as well as uncomfortably out of alignment with myself. Any 'natural presence' I could ordinarily claim had vanished. But I noticed on the conference schedule that every morning at 6:30, there was an opportunity to meditate. That felt inviting, and the next morning, I attended this session.

A husband and wife were the teachers, and they opened the small gathering with the question: why did you come to be here with us at this early hour? The first thing that came to me and what I said in answer to their question: "I came to remember that I am here; to remember that I am here." What I meant, and what they understood, was that I wanted to remain present to myself instead of losing my bearings to the energies of what was happening around me. I needed a way to gather those bearings. Sitting in this small practice circle for the remaining days at the conference became the means that I needed. It allowed me the opportunity to stay in touch with myself so that I could be more present in the parts of the program that were of interest to me. In a way, it enabled me to come home to myself and to remember how I wanted to 'be' in this experience. The grounding that I felt in those quiet sits allowed me to begin the day, having reclaimed my internal alignment without the scattered energies of feeling dislocated.

That is something I've learned that meditation can help us do; it can help us remember to come back to a HOME place, to bring us back in touch with ourselves when the world of family, job, and daily living responsibilities tries very hard to move us away. It is fundamental to our human nature, though, to forget. I had 'forgotten' while in the field of that conference atmosphere. Fortunately, in the practice of vipassana meditation, there is a saving grace when that forgetting happens. It is the simple instruction to Begin Again. When the mind wanders, as it inevitably does, teachers tell us to "Begin Again." Start over. No matter how often the attention wanders, no matter how distracted or discouraged we get, no matter how often we forget, we have the opportunity to Begin Again. In fact, that is the practice since every time we awake have forgotten or wandered. We have a moment of clarity, a moment of mindfulness, and, over time, those moments accumulate to increase the stability of presence.

When I first heard the prompt to Begin Again, I wasn't even hoping for more presence. What I felt was relief. I had already wandered so many times; learning that wandering was a usual part of the meditation practice normalized the experiences that I had been having. It gave me permission not only to be my imperfect human self but also to acknowledge that this is the way we are made: to have minds that are busy, to 'forget' our intentions, and to succumb to distractions.

It was at a Buddhist conference a few years later that I asked Joseph Goldstein, renowned meditation teacher and co-founder of The Insight Meditation Society (IMS) in Barre, Massachusetts, this question: What is the difference as a long-time meditator between your meditation experience now and my experience as a relatively recent practitioner? He responded," I probably wander away from my anchor less frequently than you do." That he still wandered on occasion felt like a confirmation of 'our mutual humanity. And that he wandered less frequently was the encouragement to continue beginning again.

Sometimes It's Like That

The meditation hall was not even the 'Days Inn' of meditation halls. It was old, drafty and crowded. I had been here before on another retreat, but that had been in the spring when the weather had been beautiful, and there were many fewer meditators attending. Now, it was mid-winter. The weather had been freezing cold, and the heating system in the hall required a blower to blast hot air into the high-ceilinged room. Blasting very loudly and unpredictably. It was not exactly conducive to serene meditation. Plus, as I said, it was crowded in there. So crowded that zabutons were edge to edge; we could hear each other breathe and there was no room to stand. Conditions were not conducive!

On the second morning of the retreat, I arrived for the early sit, situating myself while the hall was relatively empty so that I could enjoy a brief interval of peace. Soon, others began to take their places, and one young man settled himself about two rows in front of me. As it happened, the cushions on either side of him were not occupied by the time the bell signaled the beginning of the sit, and soon, he decided to take advantage of the extra room by lying down, sprawling, really, and then falling asleep. For the remainder of the sit, the blasts from the blower alternated with the snores of the sleeper. For times such as these, the instructions for meditators may include noticing the effects of the distractions on your thoughts, on your body, and on your mind state. My thoughts and mind-state were negative: annoyed by the blower, annoyed by the cramped space, annoyed by the young man's thoughtlessness for those around him. My body was tight, and though I returned to my breath time after time, I was also aware of the restless sounds of those sitting next to me who seemed equally uncomfortable. I felt relief when the bell rang to end this sit.

When I left the meditation hall, still dissatisfied with the conditions and with myself for allowing the conditions to discolor my mindstate, I walked out into gently falling snow. While we had been inside meditating, the snow had lightly covered the walkways and grounds, leaving a pristine blanket of white everywhere. I had loved snowfalls since I was a child, and as I walked to the dining hall, collecting flakes on my coat and noticing the way the trees were being trimmed in white, I was aware that my mood was shifting.

Then, breakfast:

the welcome quiet warmth of the dining hall
fresh hot eggs
the tasty biscuits I remembered when I was last here
the coffee exactly the right temperature
and the thought
Sometimes it's like that-
and
Sometimes it's like this.

The felt experience of Joy - - a delicious tickle from my throat to my heart.

The ache for home lives in all of us,
the safe place where we can go as we are,
and not be questioned.
Maya Angelou

Sangha

As I write this, Philip is leading a guided meditation on Zoom for about 30 people. This is his 340+ offering of mindfulness practices to this group. Begun at the start of the pandemic, it continues twice weekly because the participants have been so positive about the impact of these meetings. They have formed over time a sangha, a community of people who share an interest to practice and learn together from a teacher and from one another.

Sangha is a Pali word prominent in Buddhist circles meaning 'assembly,' 'company,' or 'community.' Originally, it applied to members of a monastic community, but today its application has been generalized to include groups meeting regularly to practice together. I apply the word to Philip's group because they assemble regularly, because they accompany each other as they study and practice mindfulness and because they have reported how much they appreciate the collective experience of being together.

I have found great value in participating in sanghas as well. For more than ten years now, I have met with four friends every other week. We call ourselves a sangha because we, too, accompany one another on this life's journey; we, too, assemble regularly, and we, too, find maintaining this connection a necessary support in navigating the ups and downs of living this human life. We meditate together, we 'check in' with updates on important happenings in our lives, and we rotate offering a reading, a poem or activity that has caught our attention.

I have come to see sanghas in their various forms as helpful in a way that is different from our individual pursuits of meaning and connection. There is something about a shared exploration that offers not only support but also safety and a sense of belonging to and in an experience that is greater than one's self.

Contentment

Not too long ago, I began a week-long online retreat with the aspiration of letting go of what I considered to be an obstructing, all too familiar and irritatingly nagging narrative; then, if that happened, I intended to turn toward the question that I sensed was just waiting for me underneath that obstruction. The retreat had begun on Friday afternoon, but It wasn't until later Monday that I recognized those as misguided aspirations that had clearly come from the head. In retrospect, though, the few days prior were not in vain. In fact, they now seem to have been necessary preparation for the remainder of the retreat.

That preparation began Saturday morning with my first exposure to QiGong. This discipline was offered for an hour and a half every day. I didn't miss one session all week. I, like apparently everybody else on the retreat, fell in love with the Mr.Rogers-like instructor who led these sessions, a guitar-playing 60-something ex-rock musician who introduced us yogis to the pulsing energies and gentle movements of the practice he calls embodied mindfulness. Teja, his name, taught simple exercises directed to opening 'channels' in the body, which, for me, especially affected my heart's spaciousness. Plus, unlike when I practice yoga, coordinating the breath with the movements seemed so naturally easy - - or as Teja would say - - effortless. So, I felt an ease that made the practices more inviting.

In the meantime, besides these sessions, we heard dharma talks by great teachers like Tara Brach and La Sarmiento, as well as guided meditations from other teachers. Then along came Konda Mason, delivering her dharma talk late Monday afternoon.

Konda, besides being a meditation teacher trained at Spirit Rock, is a social justice advocate. In her talk, though not particularly focused on those issues, she brought her advocate's fierceness to her message about living in a 'proximate relationship' (invoking Brian Stevenson) to the life within us.

She ended her talk by reciting Danna Fauld's poem:

<u>Go In and In:</u>

Go in and in.
Be the space between two cells,
the vast, resounding
silence in which
spirit dwells.
Be sugar dissolving
on the tongue of life.
Dive in and in,
as deep as you can dive.
Be infinite, ecstatic truth.
Be love conceived and born in union.
Be exactly what you seek,
the Beloved, singing Yes,
tasting Yes, embracing Yes,
until there is only essence;
the All of Everything
expressing through you
as you. Go in and in
and turn away from
nothing that you find.

It was those last lines, repeated in Konda's rich voice, that clarified and simplified for me my true aspiration for the retreat. Following her talk, I reflected on how affected I had been by those words and by how firmly they were spoken: go in and in and turn away from nothing you will find. Going in and in, what had I been turning away? What had I been bypassing? Until then, nothing had been appearing in my meditation that was at all related to my stated intention. I hadn't been hi-jacked by a nagging narrative, and nothing else had shown up worth pursuing. Instead, I had been kind of waiting or, I was telling myself, creating the opportunity for something to arise.

So, in the next sit, I just went 'in and in' and noticed what was there rather than what wasn't. And what I found: I found my body, a body that was feeling well, ready to be opened more, one that was responding to the QiGong exercises and was becoming increasingly spacious. A body at ease.

And with that discovery of a body at ease, in not too long a time, Jane Kenyon's poem "Otherwise" came to mind. The recognition that this was a state - - a state that might not, would not last. And then I knew my aspiration.

Kenyon's poem is a mix of moments of gratitude of blessings with the reality of impermanence. And I asked myself: how do I live in that place of holding both the awareness of life's richness now and the awareness of its temporariness?

I went outside; the days of the retreat had been so beautiful: the crisp air of fall, my favorite season, the colors so vivid in clear air; blue, blue sky, green, green grass, gold and red leaves; and the wind carrying the leaves that, as Thich Nhat Hahn has written, had allowed themselves to let go.

Going 'in and in' led to letting go into now . . .

Gratitude for being at home, seeing what is precious around me, and deeply feeling I am at home. In body, embodied, here now.

Then, on Thursday, I was in a small group session with teacher Jonathon Faust, and I related this experience to him. His response left me in tears. He said: "The Buddha was once asked, 'What is enlightenment'? And the Buddha answered that enlightenment is contentment."

And that word, contentment, was exactly my experience. Jonathan described contentment as a quict joy, 'a joy underneath all the waves. In life, there will be waves, the ups and downs, times of exuberance and times when we're feeling low. But this quiet joy, he said, this contentment, is the greatest happiness, is enlightenment.'

Otherwise

I got out of bed
on two strong legs.
It might have been
otherwise. I ate
cereal, sweet
milk, ripe, flawless
peach. It might
have been otherwise.

I took the dog uphill
to the birch wood.
All morning I did
the work I love.
At noon I lay down
with my mate. It might
have been otherwise.
We ate dinner together
at a table with silver
candlesticks. It might
have been otherwise.
I slept in a bed
in a room with paintings
on the walls, and
planned another day
just like this day.
But one day, I know,
it will be otherwise.

Jane Kenyon

Being Human

Many years ago, I was in private practice as a clinical psychologist. I had always been interested in human behavior and remember when I was writing college essays saying something naive like I wanted to study why people did the things they did, what made them tick. In a sense, looking for a cause-and-effect kind of understanding. And the state of psychology when I was in graduate school (at least clinical psychology), supported that orientation by focusing almost exclusively on the negative aspects of human behavior: psychopathology, depression, and the medical model; these were illnesses or disorders that needed treatment. We used a lot of the diagnosis of 'adjustment disorder' for the milder conditions that clients brought to therapy, implying that there was something wrong with how a person had adapted to the conditions of their lives; if unhappy in the marriage, an adjustment disorder; if having trouble at work, an adjustment disorder. It was necessary then to provide a diagnosis in order to offer therapy.

While still in practice but having an adjustment disorder of my own vis-a-vis my profession, I was offered a different view of things when I was exposed to Buddhist art as a docent at the Virginia Museum of Fine Arts (VMFA). As I studied the objects and read about the meaning behind the symbolism, I was struck enough by the pragmatism and realistic perspective on the human condition that I began to delve into the then-nascent field of mindfulness and meditation. Just as psychology was about a perspective on human behavior, so were those sculptures in the galleries.

The hook for me was that so much of what I was reading actually made sense; that whatever else these views were about, they were founded on an understanding of what it meant to be human. The whole of the human experience. That there was suffering in life, that how we related to that suffering made a difference and that there were skillful means for moving through these difficulties.

After 30+ years, what continues to sustain my interest is that mindfulness and these meditative practices are not about human disorders. In fact, the first thing that Jon Kabat-Zinn says to a new Mindfulness-Based Stress Reduction (MBSR) class is that there is more right with you than wrong with you - - even when he is dealing with hospital-referred patients. The focus becomes about what gets in the way of that inherent rightness. What we often label as wrong - - our anxiety, our depressed moods, the poor choices we may have made, our trouble in relationships - - are not so much disorders as they are sources of important information about our lives and how we are relating to our lives. Meditation and mindfulness give us means for exploring that information and for shifting that relationship by exposing what within us obscures our contentment and well-being and then developing skillful means to access that part of our being that is more joyful, kind, compassionate and equanimous.

Aggrieved

I am aggrieved. I have found the word that matches my subjective experience of this moment. For the past couple of hours, I have been mumbling to myself about a grievance with my husband perpetrated this morning, saying things to myself like, "He does this all the time" and "Why doesn't he see what he's doing?" and "He's so NOT aware!!!!" I've also been busy collecting from my memory bank other instances of this same habit of his so as to be prepared with DATA when I'm ready to talk about this. I've tried rehearsing a bit about how to bring this up in a way that doesn't sound churlish or accusatory, but it's clear I'm not quite there yet.

So, as I check in with my body and my mind state and my feeling tone, of course, what I find is that my mind is agitated, my jaw is tight, and my feeling - - well, it's not pleasant. I decided then to do something else for a while; taking my mind to a more 'wholesome' place may help the mental juices conjure a skillful, wise way to approach this 'issue' with him.

I had been re-reading Tara Brach's "True Refuge," and that's what I picked up for alternative input. I'm not long into it before I come across Tara's script for a guided reflection on "Remembering the Most Important Thing." In the script, she offers this question: "If I was at the end of my life looking back, what would be most important about how I lived today…this moment?"

Well, that was a stunner. I have to take a pause.

This hits me especially hard because, at 70+ years of age, I am acutely aware that I am much closer to the end of my life than to the beginning. There is a limited supply of those moments left. Furthermore, I very much want to tend to the quality of my days and with some chagrin, I recognize how far astray from that intention my morning has been. And over what? Was this grievance a devastating act of cruelty? No. It was a minor occurrence in a pattern of interaction that has been repeated probably thousands of times over the tenure of this relationship without, by the way, a particular sensitivity to it on my part until just recently.

So I sit for a while with this information and with this question of what would be most important about how I live for the rest of this day. I check in with my body, mind and feeling tone now and find that I am more settled in my body, even a little tired. I also have a bit of clarity in my mind about what I want to do. I will talk about this with him by sharing this whole cycle of experience from the initial trigger through the mounting irritation, to the good judgment I exercised by letting my reaction quiet for a bit, to Tara's question, to the eventual clarity. I will have my part of the conversation be about me. What happens then is in the context of the relationship, not dependent on one side having the better offense or the other admitting fault.

As to the bigger question - - the answer there is simple, in fact, it has become more and more simple as I have grown older. What is most important as I live the rest of this day or any of my future days? It's most important that I live them with kindness and with care, with as gentle a heart as I can bring to the people and circumstances that I meet - - and doing my best, with the help of my practices, to remember that there is a **most important thing**.

Doubt

We all have our wounds or stuck places or entrenched patterns of reacting. Every one of us. And every one of us has woven stories around those wounds and places. I began the untangling from one of my most frequently recurring and unhelpful patterns several years ago.

This took place at a time when I had been working on a project, one that was to take a couple of months from beginning to end and something that began as an original idea of mine. I was very excited about it even though it was something that involved a lot of details, which I was never excited about. One day, at my desk, absorbed with developing the idea and enjoying my absorption, I had a phone call from a friend. I was by this time well into the project, about half or two thirds of the way, when my friend offered a piece of feedback. A discouraging piece of feedback. It wasn't a major concern, just a pretty small thing, really, but once I was off the phone, suddenly (and it was suddenly), all of my energy left me. I slumped in my chair. Feeling defeated and heavy and lifeless.

Negative thoughts about the whole project surfaced. Thoughts like " This is going to be a huge failure. Why would anyone want to support this? What a dumb idea. Why did I think this was any good anyway? I should just forget about the whole thing." And, of course, as these thoughts circled in my brain, I felt worse and worse.

I sat in this discouraged space for a while, and then, within a few minutes, I realized how familiar it was. I had been here many times. In fact, it almost always happened when I had undertaken a project, especially one that was largely my idea and one that required that I produce something, like my dissertation, like the writing that I did for the museum, like planning a six-month-long program for an organization. There was always a point well into this kind of work when I would lose my spirit, where my energy for it died. I was then left with the prospect of having to honor my commitments to complete these projects despite the fact that I didn't have the belief in myself to do a good job or the confidence that it was a worthwhile thing to be doing. In other words, I ended up having to drag myself to the finish to push through the inertia rather than being excited to reach its conclusion.

So here I was again in this very familiar place. Because I had the time, because I had been working with mindfulness material and because I was so tired of this experience and tired of myself for being there, this time, I made a conscious decision to explore it, to be with the bodily experience of this place and to stay with the feelings. To allow whatever was there to be as it was. I just sat, and I put my attention on the sensations I was having, noticing where they were and simply experiencing them. The most prominent bodily sense was in my chest. I noted that my lungs felt empty as if there was no air in them.

I then asked myself, "What more can I know about this?" It was as if all the air had been let out of a balloon. I felt - - DEFLATED. Totally deflated - - exactly what I felt. Once I had that word, I sensed that I was on a road leading me somewhere. And I became more curious. I asked, "What thought am I believing now? What is the story here?" and the sentence "You can't do this" arose. And the voice of that thought was familiar. It was the voice of my father actively discouraging me (by this time, I was sobbing), and as I stayed with the sorrow welling up in me, I had the realization that, as a child and adolescent, I could not recall hearing the words "You CAN do this." I had not been encouraged to seek challenges, to stretch myself, and had not been told by my parents that they had confidence in me, that I could do or be anything I wanted to do or become. Instead, from the scarcity mentality of their hardships as children came to a wary and constricted view of possibilities, especially from my father, for women. The often-heard message was, "Don't reach too high, don't expect so much…it might be too hard for you."

I felt the grief - - deeply - - for whatever had been lost to me and for how hard the struggle had been to accomplish what I had accomplished. I wept until I finished weeping. It took a while.

And then I felt relief. And it seemed that sanity had returned to my mind with a new awareness.

For one thing, I learned to hold a more tender attitude toward my discouraged moments. I understood that I was conditioned early to think about possible failures instead of potential successes. And I saw the whole story of how deeply entrenched in me it was, how long I had been carrying that story within me, that it was a story from long ago and that it was just a story. A story that I no longer had to believe. I also eventually understood that my parents were protecting me with their caution. The world had not been a safe place for them; their fear for me was that I would experience disappointment should I overreach.

For another thing, I reached the point where I recognized the experience I was having as a cloud and not the whole of who I was. I saw that the cloud was only a part of the sky of awareness, not a blanket that covered everything else up. There was a blue, bright sky in there, too; I could say, "That's just a cloud in my awareness," and then I could watch it pass. And go on to complete the tasks at hand.

More importantly, though, the awareness I gained from moving through my doubt created a doorway that opened to possibilities. I discovered what was beyond the doubt: the possibility that I was capable of more than I knew, that the willingness to take risks in the world can lead to wonderful as well as scary things, and that failure is not as terrifying as living small.

Pema Chodron once said that

The difficult things provoke all your irritations and bring your habitual patterns to the surface. And that becomes the moment of truth. You have the choice to launch into the lousy habitual patterns you already have or to stay with the rawness and discomfort of the situation and let it transform you on the spot... One of the main things I work with personally is saying to myself, "This is how I am right now. I have a very short fuse, and I'm losing it. Then I ask myself, Do I want to strengthen this habit so that a year from now, my fuse is even shorter?

Impatience

Whether reading about mindfulness, listening to teachers' dharma talks, or following an app, it can sometimes seem as if there is so much to know and track that this is a complicated subject difficult to practice because there are so many possibilities. One person in a practice group was honest enough to say, "I feel overwhelmed. There is so much to pay attention to. How can we remember it all." And I would add to that: we and not feel like we've failed Mindfulness 101 if we don't. She was so great to raise the question because as I've reflected on it later, if it may seem as if all of this information is painting an ideal way of being - - if we're flexible, receptive, open, observing, non-judgmental, attuned and integrated not to mention present - - - - if we're a stable mountain, a deep ocean and spacious sky all at once, then maybe we'll be awake, aware, alert and mindful for this one moment.

All that seems impossible when put like that. At least to me. It's not possible to be aware every moment, to be present every moment, to be kind or to be compassionate all the time or to be 100% non-reactive despite our best intentions. So, I look for ways to keep things simple and doable. Here's an example of what I mean.

I have what I call my "Toaster" practice. On many mornings, I have a piece of toast for breakfast. I have a small toaster, but I prefer the kind of bread that comes in large slices so that when I put the bread in the slots in my toaster, about 1/4 to 1/3 of it sticks up past the part that heats the bread and thus won't be toasted. So, toasting this bread is a two-part effort. I first insert the bread for round one until it pops up. Then, I flip the bread upside down and put it back in the toaster for round two. (Now, I don't know if you know this about toasters, but they tend to be pretty slow at their jobs, and that's because there is a structural limitation that accounts for that. Apparently, speeding up the appliance's process would require so much more electrical power that they would blow up. This knowledge came from a deep curiosity about the slowness of toasters that was pursued one evening with someone who worked for Proctor-Silex, so I know it's true.) By the second round of toasting, my endurance is being tested. The temptation to push the eject button is very, very strong. What I do then is to become more and more intimate with that urge to push the button; where is it in my body, what thoughts am I having when that urge arises, and can I breathe through it?

I have chosen this practice, first of all, because it is available to do almost every day (sometimes Philip makes me a delicious egg sandwich so I don't have toast that day), second, because it is brief and so identifiable but mostly because one of my great challenges is patience. And that urge to push that button, that leaning into the next moment, is a practice edge for me. Bringing curiosity to impatience, how it feels to want things to happen faster, and how it feels to want to move on to the next thing according to my personal timetable is one of my ways of practicing patience. Getting to know impatience more intimately so that I can more quickly recognize it arising in other situations.

The experience I have when feeling the "urge" to push the button is akin to what Buddhist teacher Pema Chodron named Shenpa. She defines Shenpa as a form of attachment. That attachment has to do with wanting things to be other than the way they are. In my case, I wanted the toaster to be faster and not want to wait for anymore. She calls the urge to push the button the temptation to 'scratch the itch' or 'bite the hook,' the temptation to give into the discomfort of the urge. Pema writes that even though "we may experience 2 billion kinds of itches and seven quadrillion types of scratching, …there is really only one root shenpa, and that is ego-clinging, or, in my words, the "I" that has to have its way.

The important word here is the "I," This kind of practice brings awareness to how much "I" want things to be 'my' way, to fit 'my' expectations, 'my' needs, to satisfy me, my and mine. It brings to light those moments when we are all about ourselves, caught in our personal agendas. These agendas, our wanting and not wanting, have degrees of intensity, and Chodron advises that it's probably best to begin practicing with the least difficult temptations, like my toaster practice.

So, there is this urge, and the urge is sort of uncomfortable. In this case, not painful, not intolerable, but physically noticeable. There is then the choice:

push the button or not. Choose to live with the sensations of discomfort or choose to ease those sensations with that simple action of pushing the button.

As I had been reflecting on Shenpas, I became curious about how often these 'urges' occurred at times other than at breakfast, and it didn't take long to recognize that the toaster urge was not the only bait I felt during the day; not the only time I wanted either to hurry things up or change what was happening. I noticed the urge to have some of that delicious dark chocolate caramel sea salt gelato that was tempting me in the freezer. I noticed an automatic "No" appear, fortunately not expressed, to a suggestion someone made. I almost always feel the urge to ring the bell before the 30 minutes is up when leading a meditation.

It's kind of heartening to me that I found these impulses to be easy to identify once I developed the intention to bring awareness to them. Sometimes, there was only the mind movement, but often, there were clear physical sensations. For me, I noticed them in my throat and chest, and I also felt the pull to move my upper body forward. On only a few occasions were the sensations really unpleasant, and these were always accompanied by thoughts like " I DO NOT Want to do this!!!"

The fact that these are relatively easy to identify makes it possible to get familiar with our personal patterns of impulses or desires to change or to control or to want more of or less of something, i.e., to become familiar with patterns of wanting or not wanting. While every one of us has these itches or urges, they are idiosyncratic. Mine are not the same as anyone else's. Discovering where they show up can help us wake up to how pervasive our personal 'wanting' is. When we recognize how often we are at odds with our present moment experience, we may then begin to see how often that 'wanting' causes a lingering sense of dissatisfaction. This is an insight that can paradoxically lead to a more easeful relationship with our wanting natures, and the doorway into such an insight can begin with something as simple as a few mindful moments with a toaster.

<u>Allow</u>

There is no controlling life.
Try corralling a lightning bolt,
containing a tornado. Dam a
stream and it will create a new
channel. Resist and the tide
will sweep you off your feet.
Allow, and grace will carry
you to higher ground. The only
safety lies in letting it all in –
the wild and the weak; fear,
fantasies, failures and success.

Danna Faulds

Fear

I have had experiences with fear. I have been afraid of flying, I've been afraid of public speaking and I've been afraid of snakes. Still am afraid of snakes. I felt fear when I was diagnosed with cancer, and I felt fear when my mother had a stroke while I was on the phone with her. From these experiences and from practicing mindfulness and meditation, I have learned something about fear, like Lew in Shel Silverstein's poem.

George got stung by a bee and said,
"I wouldn't have got stung if I'd stayed in bed."
Fred got stung and we heard him roar,
"What am I being punished for?"
Lew got stung and we heard him say,
"I learned something about bees today."

As with George, Fred and Lew, it makes a difference in how we view our uncomfortable experiences and just as Lew learned something about bees, one way to be with our fears is to approach them and learn from them.

One of the things I've learned about fear is that being afraid is not a mistake. Whatever the fear, it's not wrong to feel the energies of anxiety, panic or shakiness. It's not a mistake because fear is a normal response of this mammalian human organism to a perceived or real threat to our safety and well-

100

being. It is a physiological response built into our nervous systems. It is one of those four things that is not our fault. It's how we're made. It's important to remember this because it helps us move away from resisting the feeling that arises when we are afraid and move toward allowing it to be there. Fighting the fear only intensifies it, constricts us more or makes us smaller and less able to move through it. We become the fear. And understanding that such reactivity is beyond our control lessens the self-judgment that we may throw at ourselves for being afraid. Judgments like, "You are you such a coward" or "Stop being such a baby!" Instead, we name it. We say, "Oh. Fear is here." Noting it in that way helps us take this experience less personally without labeling ourselves as somehow flawed or weak.

So - - fear is normal.

I've also learned that fear varies a lot. Some fears may be useful at the moment to protect us or someone we love, other fears are about opportunities to open to more of life or to more of ourselves, and still, others are fears that do not send us in a helpful direction, usually falling in the category of 'what ifs.'

My 97-year-old mother had a stroke when I was on the phone with her one morning. In the middle of a sentence, she stopped talking. All I could hear were strange gurgling sounds, and she was not responsive to my shouts at her. Fear came up in me immediately; fear that she had fallen, that she had had a stroke, that she may have died. My fear was for her safety and for her life. My fear activated a reactive response: I cried and ran to find Philip and tell him what had just happened; then, breathing and pausing a bit more responsively, I told him to call her residence and insist that someone check her apartment. I then left to be with her. But it was critical to my mother's life to have had that reactive fear pulse through me. In this case, it urged me to take action.

But that same impulsive reaction to fear would not have been of help to me as I drove to her residence and as I navigated the weeks subsequent to her stroke. This was the territory where those unhelpful fears that get to be loops of worries, projections of what might happen if…. We're ready to hi-jack me into anxiety about the future. And this is one of the many places where mindfulness has really been of value to me. Once, my mom was in the hospital from the day of her stroke and into the next few weeks, I encountered one uncertainty after another: what if she doesn't survive the night? What if she can never walk again? What if she can't talk? With the unsettling sense of not knowing what was next and the tendency to project into the future, I recognized that such thoughts only aroused anxiety in me without leading to any helpful resolution. They were useless speculations. With mindfulness, I was mostly able to become aware of those thought-trains and remind myself that uncertainty was the reality right now. Then, I could bring myself back to be grounded in the present moment.

Recognize, allow and come back to presence - - with kindness.

Asking myself: What's happening? How am I with it? What's here? And what am I bringing to it?

One more example:

Years ago, I was a person for whom speaking in public was torturous and full of fear. Jerry Seinfeld once remarked that he didn't understand why people feared public speaking more than they feared death. He didn't understand it because he'd never heard of anyone being killed by a podium. Well. What he didn't know was that the fear experienced in front of an audience can feel like you're dying. Anyway, I was one of those. But it turned out that working through that fear, meeting its edge over and over again through serving as a docent at the VMFA and through offering other programs would not have been possible if I hadn't committed to discovering more of what I could include in my experience. There came a time when I had to decide whether I was willing to endure the discomfort of the anxiety as it played out in my body in order to move toward an experience that I knew would be meaningful for me. I had to risk finding out what I had the capacity to tolerate to include in my experience; I learned that I could include the discomfort of my pounding heart, my squeezed chest muscles, and my aching jaw.

Teacher Tara Brach has said that we tend to overestimate the threat within our fears and underestimate our resources in the face of them. And she says that the limit of our freedom is what we are willing to experience. All this is to say that our experiences with fear can also be our teachers. We can come to recognize our vulnerabilities, our resources and our resilience. In fact, we can learn that our awareness is vast, without boundaries. If we contact that spaciousness, it will hold all of our experience and allow us to move through fearful moments and be more fully available to the richness of life.

******It is important to note that this discussion was not about the fear associated with PostTraumatic Stress Disorder (PTSD), or with traumatic events in general. Trauma-induced fear is on a different level and requires a special approach to releasing trauma's impact. There are some exciting new interventions in this area, and I recommend Bessel VanDer Kolk's book - - <u>The Body Keeps the Score</u> (2014) for those who are interested in finding out more about those interventions. Working with traumatic fears is best done together with a supportive person who can hold the space and serve as a guide as the fear is present.

About Thoughts

Researchers at the University of Virginia and Harvard wanted to test how happy people are while sitting alone and thinking. They placed hundreds of volunteers in sparsely furnished rooms for 'thinking periods' of from 6 to 15 minutes. No smartphones or other items. They were just supposed to think. Afterward, volunteers were very clear when questioned: they didn't like it at all, even when researchers allowed them to sit in their own homes for the study. The volunteers liked reading or listening to music twice as much as just thinking. Researchers were so surprised at how much the subjects disliked sitting alone with their thoughts they created a new thinking room; in it, subjects were given one distraction: the ability to give themselves a painful electric shock. All participants had previously stated that they would pay good money to avoid an electric shock. No one thought getting a shock was good. The subjects were simply asked to sit in an empty room for 15 minutes. The results: 25% of women and 67% of men chose to self-administer a painful electric shock rather than sit there quietly.

It's amazing how unpleasant people find it to be alone with their thoughts! (I'll leave the question of gender difference alone!!)

Then, the researchers conducted another study and introduced a different condition. They wanted to determine how mind-wandering correlated with emotional tone. They created an app for smartphones that would contact people at random intervals throughout their normal day and ask, "What are you doing? How happy do you feel? Are you focusing on what you are doing? If not, is what you are thinking about pleasant, unpleasant or neutral?" The researchers gathered more than 250,000 samples from around the world. What they found was that fun activities didn't correlate much with happiness. Instead, what mattered was whether they were paying attention to what they were doing. Focused attention was strongly correlated with feeling happy, whereas having a wandering mind was usually accompanied by unpleasant feelings. Wandering mind occurred in 50% of the samples. Apparently, when left to its own devices, the human mind is a wandering mind, and this study suggests that a wandering mind is an unhappy mind.

While there are many ways of feeling better, apparently, one of the most powerful is simply to concentrate on what you are doing in the moment. Developing the capacity to be more present, which is what mindfulness practice points toward, leads to greater well-being.

Of all the experiences we have that make being present a challenge, probably very close to the top, if not the top, is our thinking. When we begin to meditate and practice mindfulness, the first thing we encounter is our thought stream. How many times have we been carried away from the breath by a memory, a worry or a random observation? And isn't it often true that we would prefer to follow that mental distraction than return our attention to what's happening in the present moment?

It's a fact that we have brains whose job it is to generate thoughts. I've heard this fact about thoughts cited many times: it's estimated that we have about 67000 thoughts a day, and 90% of those are the same thoughts we had yesterday. If this is even close to true, then the majority of our thoughts are at the least irrelevant or very stale. Experts also report that 80-90-% of human thought comes under the heading of 'negative rumination,' meaning that it is both repetitive and disturbing in some way. Irrelevant, repetitive, disturbing and cluttered. Where is the room for creativity or new ideas?

Yet one of the facts of conditioning in our culture is that we are taught to value our rational minds and intelligence very highly. Our ability to think. Our cognitive capacity. So, we are not inclined to question much the nature of our thoughts or how the process of thinking works or shapes our reality. But that's exactly what insight meditation and mindfulness ask us to do: to look at nature and the process of our thinking, and when we do, we come to a different relationship with the 67000 mind moments we experience every day.

What might that relationship be? From the mindfulness perspective, a thought is:

- a blip of energy in the mind

- an ephemeral event of the mind; temporal, arising, appearing and vanishing
- a movement of the mind
- images, memories, fantasies, songs, dreams
- anything that the mind creates is considered to be a mental formation

There is no question that thoughts are necessary, even critical, for navigating this world. They are the source of all invention, creativity, and imagination, not to mention problem-solving and educating. We need them to live our lives on a day-to-day basis.

But without some awareness of how they influence us, we are at their mercy, and they do not always lead us in positive, wholesome directions. They can dominate our moods, limit our potential, and influence our experience of whatever is going on in at least these three ways.

Here are some of the ways that thoughts can be problematic.

1. We get lost in them. They can cloud our thinking. A good analogy here is one that I've heard Tara Brach use. Imagine you are in an airplane and you are flying through a cloud. This happened one year when Philip and I were flying to Boston in February. From the moment we took off until we landed, we couldn't see anything through the cloud cover - - for the whole entire hour-plus of the flight! That's what it's like when our thinking clouds our experience of the present moment. Contrast that to flying through the air on a day when the sky is clear and blue, and there are puffs of clouds that go by every now and then. Clouds are the thoughts that arise and pass; the sky is our awareness that notices; oh, there's a thought.

2. Another way that thoughts can be problematic is that we come to see our experience through stale frames of reference or on automatic pilot, only taking in information that reinforces what we already know or believe. We develop mind habits of opinions, beliefs and attitudes that filter our interactions so that we come to see things as we are, not as they are.

3. Thought can trap us into a spiral of painful rumination, obsessive thinking, frustration, anger or a mood of negativity and suffering. The emphasis in mindfulness is not so much on 'what' we think, the content, but on 'how'

we think, the process. We are not trying to get rid of thought but rather cultivate a way of being with thought 'artfully' so that we come to know how thoughts can serve us and direct us toward greater well-being.

4. The practices of mindfulness and meditation allow us to bring awareness to these patterns and mental habits directly so that we become mindful of the thinking process itself. And we become more awake to how thoughts can grab us, envelop us and overtake us. The benefits of practicing meditation and mindfulness include not only revealing these problematic thinking processes but also offering us a way to change our relationship to thoughts so that we are not so often carried away, not so often enamored of them, not so often thinking negatively and not so often at their mercy.

Love, Power and Separation

Adam Kahane is a consultant who has been called to many corners of the world to facilitate gatherings that aspire to cross great divides from post-civil war Guatemala to post-apartheid South Africa, to India and Israel, to countries and leaders wrestling with problems of warring factions, cultural schisms, and political stalemates. He has worked with problematic separations on the global level for more than 20 years. He writes in his book <u>Power and Love</u> that, early on, his facilitating methods were based on love: on opening and connecting with the intention of "making whole that which had become or appeared to be fragmented." But what he discovered, after reflecting on a few disappointing outcomes, was that even after love had established common ground among the various stakeholders, the unity that had been established fell apart because of the failure to take power issues into account. Kahane says,

> *I had been assuming that what was common was more important than what was different. I had seen in my own behavior... a conflict-averse love that disempowered others and denied my own power...*

Describing one unsuccessful effort in the Philippines, Kahane noted

> *we had focused most of our attention on unity, not on the different and conflicting positions and interests of the participating groups...The acrimonious collapse of the workshop agreements produced not merely failure but a regression.*

I think we would like to believe that love conquers all, that if we are caring enough, kind enough, patient enough, compassionate enough that things, whatever the separations, will be healed. That love SHOULD be enough. But Kahane quotes Martin Luther King's statement that

> *love without power is sentimental and anemic, and power without love is reckless and abusive. And... power and love have been described as the most troublesome pair of opposites that we can try to reconcile.*

This polarity between love and power separates on many levels. I recognize it's the force in my own life. I grew up in a home where children were to be seen and not heard, where girls especially were to be quiet. This was an explicit message, repeated in many circumstances by my father and embodied in the relationship between my parents. My mother was love; my father was power. No surprise then that I married power just as my mom had. Perhaps I believed that I wouldn't have to develop my own, that as a couple, we were whole, but I was young, in love, and unaware of any unconscious dynamics. It turns out that establishing my power and his corresponding movement toward love have been the great challenges of our marriage, as well as defining the growth path for each of us as individuals.

We loved each other - - yes - - though this was not enough to bridge this gap between us. His fear of vulnerability and my fear of being dismissed and diminished should I express disagreement kept us apart and fed the distance. The process of healing this separation really began within each of us. Then came finding the courage to express - - and risk disapproval or being shamed. Certainly, my first expressions of differences, of disagreement, were awkward, painful and adolescent. Like Kahane, I, too, was conflict-averse, very frightened of having my sense of worthlessness confirmed. There were many unpleasant exchanges. And Philip, on the other hand, struggled to see himself as loveable, as fundamentally good. He had to work through doubts and prickly sensitivities. It was only as we began to discover within ourselves the capacity for what the other brought to the relationship and then worked to cultivate that capacity that we were able to find a path to complete acceptance of each other.

We have, he and I, over many years, found a way to be at ease with our differences. But as Kahane found, love for each other was not enough. It took commitment, intention and a willingness to accept a share of the responsibility for the separateness. As Kahane writes:

"In healing ourselves, our wound becomes our gift. It points us to the part of ourselves that is sensitive and vulnerable and so requires our compassionate attention."

What needs to be healed also points to the part of ourselves that is conditioned and reactive. I think it is a great gift of the neurological research on meditation and mindfulness and of writers like Rick Hanson that we are learning how conditioned we are, that we are creatures of the earth, and that we have an animal nature that has protected us from threat. It offers us a way to understand our baser impulses, our tendencies to withdraw or attack; it gives us the space to be gentler with ourselves as we navigate an increasingly complex world - - or the normal strains of relationships. In offering us this allowance it also opens the door to understanding others as members of the same species. If this is how I am, so is it how others are.

In working to counter these conditioned behaviors and reactive patterns, Philip and I were and are going about the business of healing the way in which we had separated from ourselves. This is what Kahane would call a form of power: power is the drive of everything living to realize itself. The power of the human urge to individuate. My drive to find my own power; Philip's drive to touch into his Buddha nature. And that urge to individuate, to be realized, is the source of diversity that must be acknowledged in personal growth and collectively healthy communities and groups.

I am not saying that love cannot heal. Kahane didn't say that either. It's evident that love often speeds healing, that love has fostered miracle cures, and that without love, wounds may remain open and painful. But if we choose to bypass differences on the way to resolution, we are assuming a conformity that may not exist. Sometimes, it may simply be the easy way out or, as Kahane said, a risk-averse path.

Whether we call it love and power, or any other pair that names this difference - - male-female, honesty and kindness, clarity and compassion - - it is about bringing all of what IS to the table, shining the light of awareness on the parts, acknowledging, respecting, allowing them to mix it up while holding them in a container of intention and caring. Each must feel its own integrity, find its own voice, speak its own truth, and, in the cacophony, create a reality that will honor its participation.

So, in addition to love's essential ingredient for healing, we are reminded of Nelson Mandela's quote from Marianne Williamson in his presidential inaugural speech:

..when we let our own light shine, we unconsciously give other people permission to do the same. As we are liberated from our own fear, our presence automatically liberates others.

Park Practice

We've been in Maine now for three weeks, and it's been great! One of my pleasures here is that each morning, early, I take one of our dogs for a walk through the 100-year-old city park that's a short distance from where we're staying. For the past several days, I've introduced a simple mindfulness practice into this daily habit. As I start up the hill from our house, I say the mantra, "May I be more mindful today." I repeat it a few times at the beginning, and then, if I remember, I repeat it later as I'm heading back toward the cup of coffee waiting for me.

This simple practice has been a good reminder of a few key points. First, it's not too difficult to be mindful when you are alone with your dog on a beautiful morning in Maine. There might be fog to feel or pinkish light to notice or the Art Deco filagree on the park entrance to appreciate. The cool temperature invites stopping to experience the sensations on the skin, and my dog's frequent pauses to sniff that allow me to pause and breathe as well. Yes, mindfulness, especially when the intention has been explicit and then joined with an already established routine, can itself become automatic.

Until...

People are involved.

One morning, a friendly woman approached me as I was walking up the street, saying my mantra. She introduced herself and said she was a new resident in the neighborhood and thought I might be a neighbor that she hadn't yet met. We chatted briefly, then each went on our way. And despite having the intention to be mindful, to be present to my experience as it was happening, I promptly forgot her name. An indication that something else was holding my attention when she said her name. As I thought about this, I realized that my mind was so busy manufacturing questions (Why is she coming towards me? Who does she believe me to be? Is she going to ask me something? etc.) that I didn't even hear her name. And then was too embarrassed later to ask her to repeat it. So, I was otherwise occupied. Not a terrible thing in itself. It happens often. But I was reminded of how easily I can cloud a moment with my own concerns and that being fully present means holding both the internal and external experience, the whole of it.

This morning's walk brought another kind of mindful moment to my attention. My dog and I were in the park. She sniffed, noticing the handsome old trees around us, when a couple jogging with their dog appeared in view. As soon as my dog saw their dog, my dog began barking and continued to bark. As the couple moved past us, I heard the man mumble under his breath. I thought he made a negative remark about my "yapping" dog. (Theirs was not barking.) For the next few minutes, I found myself spinning stories and conjuring negative thoughts ("Really? Their dog doesn't bark?"). It didn't take me too long to recognize how I was the one ruining my quiet time. When I did, I could then let go and return to being in the park rather than in my head.

Where was the mindfulness in this encounter? It came after the event: in the noticing of my internal reaction, in becoming aware of the thoughts my mind was generating and in recognizing how those thoughts were affecting my experience in the moment.

One of my favorite Zen authors, Ezra Bayda, when in the midst of a difficult circumstance, asks himself the question: "How is this a part of the path?" In a similar way, I can take small 'lapses', such as those I've described, as opportunities to reinforce my intention and/or to learn more about my reactive patterns. One of the benefits of this practice is that when I become aware of and accept the inevitable moments of mindlessness, I can see them as possibilities to become more awake instead of believing them to be 'mistakes' for which I must judge myself negatively.

Intention helps.

Lapses happen.

Mindfulness accumulates.

About (UN)Wise Speech

Rabbi Rami Shapiro writes of an Hasidic teaching that each of us is born with a fixed number of words to speak, and when we have spoken the last of these, we die. Rabbi Rami then asks, "How would your everyday speech change if you really believed that?"

It's a question worth pondering. How WOULD your everyday speech change if you knew that you had only so many words - - an unknown quantity - - to speak in this life and that you would die when those words were used up?

Many of us are familiar with the classic standards for wise speech:

Is it true?
Is it beneficial?
Is it kind?
Is it necessary?

But what comes to mind for me is that Rabbi Rami's question suggests that we should also consider all the qualities of unwise speech, the opposites of those standards. Unwise speech includes:

- Lying: speech with the intention to deceive. This includes exaggeration, little white lies, insincere comments, and even withholding of truth.

- Maliciousness: speech with the intention to create rifts, division and discord

- Harshness: speech with the intention to hurt another, including tone of voice, sarcasm, swearing and loudness

- Frivolousness: speech with the intention to draw attention, idle chatter, gossip, empty words, "junk food for the ego."

To shake ourselves awake from "slumbering on the pillow of our unconscious" (Thomas Moore), we can be willing to be more open, to be purposely more noticing. In fact, Harvard professor Ellen Langer, who has researched mindfulness for decades, claims that all it takes to live mindfully is to look for the new, whether walking, or driving or gazing at a friend; just look for what you haven't seen before.

We also can intentionally widen our perspectives. If we learn to step back some distance from our own thinking and judging processes, we can untangle ourselves from our typical enmeshments, not necessarily to rid ourselves of them but to hold them more lightly. We can then 'see our own seeing.' Widening introduces those questions I mentioned earlier: What else is here? Is there another way of thinking about this?

And we can deepen. This has to do with personal probing, with learning what sabotages, diverts or distorts our consciousness.

But none of these avenues is easy. The most important work we can do is to try to ensure that the actions we choose throughout our day are skillful. This is not simply a question of observing a series of rules but of actively working to ensure that our vision and discernment is as clear as it can be. If we are not aware, we are acting out of conditioning: the same old, same old. If we are able to see more clearly, we have a greater opportunity of acting skillfully.

A Buddhist scripture teaches this lesson in negativity: Do not be a person who adds to the thoughtlessness of the time. We can take our capacities for directing our attention and for expanding this gift of awareness seriously; we can use our practices to become more alert and awake to our own arenas of blindness so that we add to the consciousness rather than to the thoughtlessness of our time.

When you meet your friend on the roadside or in the marketplace,
Let the spirit in you move your lips and direct your tongue.
Let the voice within your voice speak to the ear of his ear;
For his soul will keep the truth of your heart
as the taste of the wine is remembered
When the color is forgotten and the vessel is no more.
Kahlil Gibran

What Are You Willing To See?

Typically, we see through the veils of our collective histories, through the veils of our conditioning, through the unquestioned beliefs that we carry, through the preferences and expectations that we have, through whatever it is that generally preoccupies our minds. Actually, that word, PRE-occupies, says it clearly. When our mind space is already occupied, there's no room for anything new. In fact, it may not be possible for any one of us to see without these influences pulling us from time to time in one direction or another, without these misconstruing brains convincing us that things are one way versus another. But we can become aware that we do have these biases, these veils.

And that's why the question - - what are you willing to see - - is important.

Here is the experience that provoked this topic.

The Virginia Museum of Fine Arts (VMFA) sponsored a series during one summer that featured meditation to go along with an exhibit of Tibetan Buddhist art. Philip and I were asked to lead one of these sessions. Since ours was the first session in the series and we were uncertain about how experienced the audience would be with meditation, we decided to do a basic introduction to mindfulness. As a part of my piece, I used a quotation that I had said many times before and had always liked. Describing the busyness of the human mind, author Annie LaMott wrote that her mind was like a bad neighborhood; she wouldn't want to go there alone. As usual, the quotation received a laugh and the rest of the program proceeded and was well received. After we had ended, people were coming up to us with comments, and one woman, a person of color, waited to speak with me. After introducing herself, she said, and I am trying to quote her as accurately as I remember, "It would sure be nice to see more faces of color here. People in those bad neighborhoods you spoke about need these practices, too."

What are you willing to see?

This woman's words have stayed with me.

So what had I seen when I first sat in front of an audience of more than 100 people at the museum? I saw friends sitting a few rows up; I saw mostly white, older women, and I saw them through my somewhat nervous lenses and thought: Oh. I know these people. They are familiar to me. I have spoken to them before. It will be okay. I saw what was known to me and was seeing through my ego's need to calm my anxiety.

Author Thomas Moore has said, "We all live in our palaces of ignorance," and the woman's words had revealed to me an aspect of my ignorance. I felt embarrassed that I had used that story so many times without consideration of how it might be heard 'across differences.' I felt sadness and irritation with my own blindness and then became aware that I had no idea of the depth of that blindness and the size of that palace of ignorance.

'What am I willing to see?' became a question that I held for the rest of the summer. This awareness of ignorance also led to a number of questions that I brought into my meditation and periods of contemplation when I noticed myself judging, being critical, and feeling resistant; questions like 'What else is here? Is that really so? Is there another way? Maybe what I see or think I know is not the whole picture.'

Without meditation training and dedicated practice, it is very difficult to see life clearly. We work with tainted data and incomplete information, even in the simplest transactions and interactions. Trying our best to see clearly so that we can act ethically and honorably is some of the toughest but most useful inner work that we can do.

Each of us has his or her own internal set of obstacles that interferes with growing our conscious awareness. The more we learn about what they are, the more we seek to free ourselves through those obstacles, and the more able we will be to see with what Emily Dickinson called "the unfurnished eye."

While the particular example that I have shared concerns my blindness to the experience of persons of color, there are other areas in which it may be hard for us to be willing to see clearly. Whenever we hold different perspectives, different beliefs, and strong emotional reactions, there is the chance that we will resist the opportunity to look past or below our own set views to ask whether there is more to know.

To shake ourselves awake from "slumbering on the pillow of our unconscious" (Thomas Moore), we can be **willing** to be more open, to be purposely more noticing. In fact, Harvard professor Ellen Langer, who has researched mindfulness for decades, claims that all it takes to live mindfully is to look for the new, whether walking, or driving or gazing at a friend; just look for what you haven't seen before.

We also can intentionally widen our perspectives. If we learn to step back some distance from our own thinking and judging processes, we can untangle ourselves from our typical enmeshments, not necessarily to rid ourselves of them but to hold them more lightly. We can then 'see our own seeing.' Widening introduces those questions I mentioned earlier: What else is here? Is there another way of thinking about this?

And we can deepen. This has to do with personal probing, with learning what sabotages, diverts or distorts our consciousness.

But none of these avenues is easy. The most important work we can do is to try to ensure that the actions we choose throughout our day are skillful. This is not simply a question of observing a series of rules but of actively working to ensure that our vision and discernment is as clear as it can be. If we are not aware, we are acting out of conditioning: the same old, same old. If we are able to see more clearly, we have a greater opportunity of acting skillfully.

A Buddhist scripture teaches this lesson in negativity: *Do not be a person who adds to the thoughtlessness of the time*. We can take our capacities for directing our attention and for expanding this gift of awareness seriously; we can use our practices to become more alert and awake to our own arenas of blindness so that we add to the consciousness rather than to the thoughtlessness of our time.

The Question Of What To Do

I had been on a silent meditation retreat at a retreat center for four days when I noticed her one morning. She was unusual even in this collection of the sometimes off-beat, not quite mainstream meditators. It was at breakfast, and she wore sunglasses indoors. Her sweater was on backward, and she was chewing gum. No one else chewed gum. Her clothes were odd: a wild scarf tied around her waist, a long, sagging skirt and leggings, all mismatched. She caught my eye because she was the only person at the buffet, and I hadn't noticed her at all in the past few days. When there is little else to do but sit and walk in silent meditation, you tend to become familiar with at least the outlines of the others who are on this path with you.

So, having finished my breakfast, I watched her for a few minutes as she struggled with the plastic tongs to lift a piece of bread onto her plate. She dropped whatever she had grasped with the tongs at least 2 or 3 times. And she didn't move from that particular spot in the buffet line. Other late arrivals just stepped in front of her to fill their plates with the eggs and blintzes that were further down the table. Every now and then, I saw her pause, look up and around, scanning the room. From a distance, it seemed that she was frozen there, unable to take from the table what she wanted and unable to move forward without it.

Though aware that on retreat, the purpose is to focus on one's own business, I was touched by this woman's seeming predicament, and I reached a point of wondering whether I should offer my help. She did seem to need some kind of assistance. But I have made such offers before only to discover that my perception of the situation was mistaken, and I, and the person I thought needed help, ended up embarrassed.

I left my seat, cleared my breakfast dishes and paused to think. I decided that if she was still in that same spot when I turned around, I would make an offer of some kind to her. When I saw that she hadn't yct moved, I walked over and stood beside her. I noticed that she had piled 3 or 4 large pieces of bread on her plate, along with perhaps a dozen butter patties. She was now holding the jam jar in her hand. I knew that opening the jam had been problematic for others, so I whispered, "Can I help you?" She looked at me - - a little stunned, I think, to hear a voice in this otherwise silent dining room - - and said, "I was just….just…". I said, "I will hold the jam for you." But when I put my hand out to take the jar, she clenched her grip. "I was just….just….," she repeated.

I may have misread this, but there seemed to be fear in her eyes, and I knew at that moment as I looked at her that offering to help was the wrong thing to do. I wished later that I had apologized and given her a little bow before I walked away, but I didn't. I was instead caught in the self-consciousness of my mistake.

Compassion can be a tricky business. When faced with someone else's pain, the natural response is to reach out, to ease the suffering, to do something. But the wise response to the arising of compassion often requires discernment and caution. It was evident that my noticing her at all had been an invasion. She, more than anything wanted to remain hidden behind her sunglasses.

In the Buddhist tradition, compassion is described as the quivering of the heart in response to another's suffering. It is recognizing that pain is a part of our human condition, mine and yours. And it is a call to ease that pain. However, the action taken must be in context and follow from an internal assessment of one's own intentions and assumptions. Of course, sometimes it is obvious what needs to happen. A child falls down and cries; a mother checks on the injury and offers comfort. Emergencies require quick responses. But many situations are not so obvious.

At a time in our world when images of suffering fill our TV screens and newspapers, when we see rivers of people wading through the mud toward the hope of a safer life when we watch those stricken with grief stack flowers high up a wall, our hearts do quiver in response to the suffering. But what do we do? What action do we take?

The reality is that sometimes we must live with the knowledge that there is nothing that we can do and that no effort of ours can alleviate a particular suffering. Sometimes, as was true for me, we simply will not know what it is best to do. Yet, we need not lose that moment of compassion. We can always strengthen the intention to remain open to possibilities and not turn away when we encounter suffering. We can always practice feeling in our softened hearts. And we can always direct that quivering energy of our caring into a random act of kindness.

Empathic Distress

For any of us who has had a loved one go through an emotionally difficult experience, we are faced with an emotionally challenging experience of our own. How can we manage our own inevitably complicated feelings and be of effective assistance at the same time?

I've been thinking about this a lot lately. My reflections have brought to mind a well-known mindfulness quote that says "What good is a clear mind if not wedded to a tender heart?" This refers, of course, to the importance of practicing meditation and mindfulness with a gentle and kind acceptance of our own and others' personal human vulnerabilities. But sometimes, especially when loved ones in distress are involved, we forget that the reverse is also of value:"What good is a tender heart if not wedded to a clear mind?"

Without that clear mind, we can easily be caught in our own distress into taking unskillful action. When our hearts have been flooded with pain, we may act out of our own suffering to alleviate our pain rather than discern the wisest course of action.

As I was exploring this topic, I came across a discussion of "empathic distress" on UC Berkeley's Greater Good Science Center website... Empathic distress is described there as "an emotional state characterized by an inability to tolerate the perceived pain or suffering of another."

It is a condition in which the distress experience has been mirrored; the empathizer, in effect, takes on the other's distress, feels the same feelings as the other and then directs their actions toward reducing their own discomfort because it is too painful to bear. Jumping into wanting to fix things, immediately trying to rescue, sending more money, acting out of fear.

While empathy, defined as the ability to put ourselves in the shoes of another person, is important for understanding another's emotions, when we SHARE the suffering of others too much, our own negative emotions increase. A recent study found that the "empathic" brain network, when lighted up, is the same network associated with pain perception and unpleasantness. In contrast, the compassionate brain network is associated with love and affiliation. When subjects were trained in compassion skills through loving kindness meditations, changes occurred in the way their brains processed distressing scenes. Negative emotions did not disappear, but individuals were less likely to feel distressed by them, which allowed for being with a negative emotion from a calmer mindset.

In another study, Matthieu Ricard, who has been called the 'happiest man in the world,' was first taken through a series of exercises focusing on eliciting empathy," feeling the feelings of suffering individuals depicted in images; in a second study, he was asked to generate compassion for similar images of suffering. He reported afterward that he became despondent after the empathy series but felt much more positive after the compassion series.

What's the difference?

When we empathize and feel 'with' a person who is suffering, we SHARE their feelings; when we feel 'for' a person who is suffering, we may feel concerned, but we do not feel the same feelings. In other words, our experience involves less identification, less merging with and into the experience of the other, allowing more for the possibility of bringing a clear mind state into our decision-making of what to do next.

Knowing when to step back in the face of suffering is an offering to yourself of the breathing space needed to garner your inner resources of balance and calm. You are recognizing that the clarity needed to respond in an effective way is momentarily lost. A compassionate and wise response is not born on the ground of panic. Instinctively, we reach out to shield our loved ones from pain, to protect them from hurt, but life continues to teach us that our power has limits. Compassion to act with wisdom to relieve suffering whenever possible and equally to embrace the limits of your agency and power... To be a refuge for another, you must remain connected with the truth of their pain and remain unflinching in the face of that truth.

Christina Feldman

When compassion includes the wisdom of clear seeing, of being with the truth of the moment unencumbered by personal needs or preferences, that is equanimity.

123

Resourcing

I am not a natural cheerleader. I'm not fond of affirmations, for instance. I don't watch the Hallmark Channel either. I think it's my Finnish background that doesn't admit much sentimentality. I tend to see myself as a realistic optimist rather than a romantic, But that reserve doesn't save me from becoming overwhelmed sometimes by the news when something tragic or terrifying happens. And these events erupt randomly, without forewarning, catching us off guard- yet by now also not quite surprised. Stunned perhaps at the senselessness or callousness that we witness, we have been faced with a relentless shower of awful events recently. (And I have realized that it doesn't matter when this was written. It will be true no matter how many months or years elapse before this is read.)

Though we often talk about the difficult and facing the hard things so that we can move through them towards a space that allows us to respond with wisdom, there is another way to move these experiences, and that is by deliberately opening the door to experiencing the joyous and the positive possibilities that life offers us.

We can adopt a perspective and a set of attitudes that enable our vision to see and savor moments that are beautiful, enlivening, joyous, and uplifting. In fact, this is necessary so that we don't lose the capacity for appreciation, for pleasure, for awe.

As most of you know by now, I often look to poetry to help me find a way when being with the difficult events that living on this planet in this peculiar and unprecedented time has challenged our possibilities of thriving.

<u>Sometimes</u>

Sometimes when day after day we have cloudless blue skies, warm
temperatures, colorful trees and brilliant sun, when
it seems like all this will go on forever,
when I harvest vegetables from the garden all day,
then drink tea and doze in the late afternoon sun,
and in the evening one night make pickled beets
and green tomato chutney, the next red tomato chutney,
and the day after that pick the fruits of my arbor
and make grape jam,

when we walk in the woods every evening over fallen leaves,
through yellow light, when nights are cool, and days warm,

when I am so happy I am afraid I might explode or disappear
or somehow be taken away from all this,

at those times when I feel so happy, so good, so alive, so in love
with the world, with my own sensuous, beautiful life, suddenly

I think about all the suffering and pain in the world, the agony
and dying. I think about all those people being tortured, right now, in
my name. But I still feel happy and good, alive and in love with the
world and with my lucky, guilty, sensuous, beautiful life because,

I know in the next minute or tomorrow all this may be
taken from me, and therefore I've got to say, right now,
what I feel and know and see, I've got to say, right now,
how beautiful and sweet this world can be.

David Budbill

125

What's Not Wrong

When the outside world seems hazardous or crazy, we can hope for refuge in the more controlled surroundings of our personal lives. But in reality, there are no guaranteed respites from personal challenges. I know that during the initial days of the pandemic when we were still wondering whether we should risk a trip to the grocery store, Philip and I faced some of those personal challenges. First, we lost our sweet dog. She had been a part of our family for thirteen years, and she was my constant companion, especially since we had been mostly housebound. Then, a few weeks later, one of our very dearest friends - - we'd known him for almost 50 years- - passed away after suffering a very difficult illness.

To navigate that unsettling time, in some ways, it helped to be as old as I am. I've lived through the historically crazy times of the '60s when armed national guards patrolled the campus where Philip was in graduate school. There were race riots not far from my hometown and disturbances over the Vietnam War. I've experienced the deaths of both of my parents and a significant illness of my own. From this history, I at least know that I've managed to weather both cultural and personal difficulties. That offers some perspective.

Reminders of that perspective have served as a resource for me. In the context of mindfulness, that perspective has to do with asking myself to notice how I am oriented toward or disposed toward the events that have happened, that is, how I am relating to them. Just asking the question reveals the degree to which something has agitated me or saddened me. And gives me time to process what is going on within me. If I open to and allow whatever the feelings are, I can eventually arrive at acceptance, the disposition or attitude that has seemed to help me the most. Accepting that right now, it's like this. Whether sadness over the losses or worries about the virus, noting how I am affected by those events in the present moment and then adding; if it's like this right now, what are my choices?

While it's not always easy to get there, Judy Brown's poem, Trough, reminds me that sometimes we need to ride things out, to allow the flow of life to hold us, to rest there until the changes that inevitably will happen in that flow, and in us, allow us to see more clearly what we need or whether there is anything that we can contribute.

Trough

There is a trough in waves,
a low spot
where horizon disappears
and only sky
and water
are our company.

And there we lose our way
unless we rest,
knowing the wave will bring us
to its crest again.

There we may drown
if we let fear
hold us within its grip and shake us
side to side,
and leave us flailing, torn, disoriented.

But if we rest there
in the trough,
in silence,
being with
the low part of the wave,
keeping our energy and
noticing the shape of things,
the flow,
then time alone
will bring us to another place
where we can see
horizon, see the land again,
regain our sense
of where we are,
and where we need to swim.

Judy Brown

127

When I am in that space of resting in the trough and being with the low part of the wave, I am not making things worse by fighting or resisting the sadness I might be feeling, for example. I am allowing what is. And the perspective of my years lets me trust that I can weather this, too, and that I will see land again.

There's another practice that's been helpful to me during the time when so much that was happening seemed wrong or upside down. I've remembered the advice that beloved Zen master Thich Nhật Hanh offered. He suggested that

We should learn to ask, "What's not wrong?" and be in touch with that... there are so many elements in the world and within our bodies, feelings, perceptions, and consciousness - so many things that are wholesome, refreshing and healing... If we block ourselves, if we stay in the prison of our sorrow or pain or worry, we will not be in touch with these healing elements.

Wherever we are, any time, we have the capacity to enjoy the sunshine, the taste of coffee in the morning, the voice of a dear friend...We don't have to travel anywhere else to do so. We can be in touch with these things right now.

So, on a morning walk: "What's not wrong?" - - the soft breeze, the gorgeous pink of the impatiens, the happy sniffing of my dog...

This question, 'What's not wrong?' is a way to remain open to what else there is right now, in this moment, apart from the difficult circumstances beyond our control. There are possibilities for "refreshing and healing" experiences available in everyday life. The key to accessing them is we have to remain available to them, to make sure there is space in our hearts to notice them and take them in. When we ask, 'What's not wrong?' it serves as a reminder to be alert for one of those 10,000 joys that may be waiting to be noticed. It creates an opportunity to experience gratitude for whatever arises in answer to that question. And gratitude, researchers have discovered, is a healing experience.

Somewhere, I came across this Dr. Seuss quote:

Being in a slump is never much fun
And unslumping yourself is not easily done.

And what unslumps me will not necessarily unslump someone else. It takes intention to make any internal shift. And it takes giving yourself permission to unslump in the way that works best for you. I have friends who find their centers when they are digging in the dirt of their gardens others when singing or playing the piano. Others in camping or running long distances.

Any of those choices is something that's not wrong. And is something that is nourishing and something that helps the heart stay open. And something to be grateful for.

Optimist

There is a fundamental belief underpinning mindfulness: that we have a mostly unrecognized capacity for a larger way of being. Jon Kabat-Zinn puts it this way: we think we're small compared to who we really are. He says we get caught in the personal pronouns of I, my, me, and mine, and we are constricted when we do that, confined by our wants and needs to have things a certain way. It's made me think of some of my favorite lines from poetry, lines meant for every one of us even though they were written centuries ago by Hafiz.

> *You are a divine elephant with amnesia*
> *Trying to live in an ant*
> *Hole.*
> *Sweetheart, O sweetheart*
> *You are the sun in*
> *Drag!*
> Hafiz

It is optimistic, isn't it, this foundational belief that we already have everything we need to become more awake and more aware, to become more the whole of who we are. That we are enough.

I think we'd like to believe that that not only are we enough as we are but that we have an inner well of kindness and compassion and goodness that far outweighs the pettiness, the misdeeds, and the regrettable words we might have said. Sometimes, after these years of practice, I can glimpse that possibility of a bigger self within me, but sometimes I cannot.

The fact of the matter is that, in this human embodiment, we are hardwired with a negativity bias, and that bias is not our fault. That bias comes with having a primitive part of our brain that is neurologically prepared to look for threats and dangers. Not only that, some of us are genetically pre-disposed to be more vigilant or melancholic; some of us were raised in families where pessimistic or critical attitudes prevailed. We had no control over these factors either. But these factors make it even more difficult to believe that we are "the sun in Drag."

For those who are like me, doubting from time to time that you are enough, that you are the sun in drag, I wanted to share what has accounted for my trust in the mindfulness teachings for more than 25 years: the trust that allows me to consider the chance that 'enoughness' applies to me as well as to everyone else. And it's pretty simple.

Mindfulness and its practices are founded on a profound understanding of the human condition. That's the very basis of these practices. In that sense, as human beings, mindfulness helps us cultivate a clearer knowing of our humanness. We come to understand that our mind wanders and can seem out of control; we learn that we often want things to be different than they are, that we want more control than is possible, that judgments arise by the second, that often we would rather be comfortable than sit with things that are hard. And we become familiar with those doubts that our practice is leading anywhere, doubts that the core of who we are is wise and compassionate.

Within the principles and practices that make up the field of mindfulness, there is an understanding that as humans, we are subject to all of these tendencies and to those obstacles of grasping, aversion, restlessness, laziness and doubt. And that these are the very tendencies that cover our sense of enoughness. But the practice of mindfulness does not ask us to believe in our enoughness just because it says so. Instead, we are invited to discover these realities for ourselves. And over the years and with practice, I have done that part. I have discovered how vulnerable I am to the very obstacles that mindfulness names, like grasping after things like being averse to unpleasant experiences. And I've found how those obstacles only make things more difficult. And how being with and staying with the difficult relieves the struggle and allows me to move on. So, the practice has verified part one.

And if the practices lead to recognizing those qualities as aspects of this human life, and of my life - - if reveals those truths - - then possible it can also reveal what's underneath all that. I can say that practice has also offered glimpses of "the more than." That's what I tell myself when doubts arise. That

I have some way to go but that, so far at least, I have found nothing untrue about this path, and I have experienced moments of enoughness. And even a few times, I have experienced a deep connection to the universe that is far more than that. That's my evidence.

> *Forget about enlightenment*
> *Sit down wherever you are*
> *And listen to the wind singing in your veins.*
> *Feel the love, the longing, the fear in your bones.*
> *Open your heart to who you are, right now,*
> *Not who you would like to be,*
> *Not the saint you are striving to become,*
> *But the being right here before you, inside you, around you.*
> *All of you is holy.*
> *You are already more and less*
> *Than whatever you can know.*
> *Breathe out,*
> *Touch in,*
> *Let go.*
> John Welwood

Keepers

In this process of aging, I am becoming more and more aware every day of things about my body or my mind that are not the same as they used to be. I tire more easily. My blood pressure is too high. My word-finding problems aren't getting any better etc., etc. And this doesn't cover my concerns about my husband's health or my thoughts about how I would manage without him. Then there is that unpredictable, chaotic, often alarming outside world. Given so many potential causes of disquiet, I am grateful for the practices of mindfulness. They have taught me that if I dwell in the negative, if I spend a lot of time worrying, I am only strengthening negative brain circuitry, thus inviting it to occur more frequently. On the other hand, my practice has also made me aware that avoidance of the negative merely bypasses realities that I can't escape. There is then a need for finding some sort of balance, for allowing the truth of things to be known so that wise actions can be taken as needed while at the same time not becoming lost in despair by the distresses that naturally occur in life.

That's why I think 'Keepers' are important. 'Keepers' are small moments of peace, well-being, and joy that may be overlooked if we do not open ourselves to noticing them. Poet Joyce Sutphen introduced the concept of Keepers to me with her poem titled "The Book of Hours." In it, she honors singular points in time that, while perhaps seeming ordinary to you and me, nevertheless to her were vivid and meaningful.

> *There was that one hour sometime*
> *in the middle of the last century.*
> *It was autumn, and I was in my father's*
> *woods building a house out of branches*
> *and the leaves that were falling like*
> *thousands of letters from the sky.*
>
> *And there was that hour in Central Park*
> *in the middle of the seventies.*
> *We were sitting on a blanket, listening*
> *to Pete Seeger singing "This land is*
> *your land, this land is my land," and*

the Vietnam War was finally over.

I would definitely include an hour
spent in one of the galleries of the
Tate Britain, looking up at the
painting of King Cophetua and
the Beggar Maid, and, afterwards
the walk along the Thames, and

I would also include one of those
hours when I woke in the night and
couldn't get back to sleep thinking
about how nothing I thought was going
to happen happened the way I expected,
and things I never expected to happen did - -

just like that hour today, when we saw
the dog running along the busy road,
and we stopped and held on to her
until her owner came along and brought
her home - - that was an hour well
spent. Yes, that was a keeper.

The poet has inspired me to notice 'Keepers' of my own. I want to register similar moments of savoring, appreciation, and pleasure. I want them to be on call for me, to remind me that life is more than painful headlines, more than personal disappointments, more than diminished energy. There is convincing evidence that our human mind has no trouble holding on to instances of suffering but that it needs help in registering what gladdens us. I want keepers to remind me that I can balance my outlook by remembering special 'hours' of living that filled me with warmth and touched my heart. Such as.......

when Conor, now 20, was about 2 1/2
he, sitting on the floor of the entry way to his new house
calling to me as I was coming down the stairs
"Kadie" he calls- come look!
He is pointing at the pretty colors on his arm,
a tiny rainbow there and then more rainbows on his shirt
I sit next to him on the floor and find rainbows on my arms
We find them on each other - - his nose, my cheek
decorated by the fractured light shining through beveled windows

both of us shining with delight

Another time

Driving home from Florida with my Mom.
She was coming for a visit.
There was not too much traffic on I 95;
We were on a long stretch with the radio on
and it played a song we both knew.
My mom began to sing... and I began to sing along with her.
She harmonized to my melody.
The sound was sweet to me.

And this treasured moment

He shows his watching children
how to hug someone
you love a lot.
"Like this," he says.

His arms spread wide
reach out to me.
The boy he was
still in his smile.

My son's embrace
arrests my heart
this ordinary day.
Unbidden, freely given
A mother's joy.

My heart is saying Thank You.

P.S. So is my body.

Country Walking

I have been walking with dogs for more than forty years. We have had eight of these companions ranging in size from labs to a miniature schnauzer. All have been wonderful pets, and all have been great walking partners.

When we lived in the country, I walked with our two dogs most afternoons. We always walked the same path: down our driveway and along the gravel road that led to our house. We covered about half a mile going out and the same half-mile coming back. And we did this hundreds of times.

I never knew what aspect of this short journey would call my attention. Sometimes, I noticed the crunch of my shoes on the ground, and I'd decide on that day to place my attention on the sounds around me. Then I heard the birds whistling, cackling, peeping, singing, so many different bird sounds that I wondered how they could tell who was talking to whom. Several times, on windy days, I noticed that trees talk, too and not just by whispering as the wind moves through the leaves. Trees whistled and groaned. They crackled and hummed. I loved standing in a certain spot along the way where there was the most conversation, eavesdropping among the tall pines and skinny hardwoods.

On another day, the plant life might catch my eye. The sunflowers in bloom! The tiger lilies bowed and spent. That delicate white blossom that opened so close to the ground. And were those black-eyed Susans there last summer?

As often as my dogs and I walked this way, there was only one summer that I saw a handsome red fox. On the first sighting, he crossed the road in front of me, stopped for a moment, seemed to measure our distance, and then continued on his way to disappear in the underbrush. Though it unusual to see a wild animal out and about in the daylight, I was told, after a second sighting, that foxes like to hunt when a storm is gathering, as it was on the two days I had spotted him. Who knew?

And then of course, I loved to watch my dogs. The elder girl, a gorgeous Vizsla, was trustworthy and didn't need to be leashed. Her explorations took her deeply into the woods or rambling through the tall meadow grass. She flushed wild turkeys, chased little rabbits, sniffed hollow trees and rolled in smelly mounds. Her enjoyment, the dog being just a dog, was a pleasure to see. The small young Schnauzer was on a leash. After all, she came to us only because she had run away from her first home and ended up being rescued by the SPCA, so she was not reliable. But watching her was fun, too. Her specialty was sniffing, moving from one attractive scent to another, wagging her stubby tail when something was especially exciting. Or she might pause, her posture suddenly erect, ears perked, head cocked, listening to a distant animal cry.

On some days, I chose to place my attention on my body as I walked. A gentle breeze might brush my skin with a temperature and touch so mild that it seemed to caress my arms...A lovely sensation.

Every day was a different day. We might have been gone for 15 minutes or 45 minutes. There was snow. There was rain. But if I was intentional when I started out, choosing where I wanted to place my attention on the walk, I almost always was rewarded with seeing something new.

<u>Going to Walden</u>

It isn't very far as highways lie.
I might be back by nightfall, having seen
The rough pines, and the stones, and the clear water.
Friends argue that I might be wiser for it.
They do not hear that far-off Yankee whisper:
How dull we grow from hurrying here and there!

Many have gone, and think me half a fool
To miss a day away in the cool country.
Maybe. But in a book I read and cherish,
Going to Walden is not so easy a thing
As a green visit. It is the slow and difficult
Trick of living, and finding it where you are...

Mary Oliver

Satisfaction

When my Mom was still well enough to take day trips, she and I often had lunch at a favorite restaurant. On one such occasion, the meal each of us had chosen was simple: a salad (mine Asian, hers more eclectic), water for a beverage and one breadstick apiece. I mention the particulars because of their ordinariness, food that appears on menus almost anywhere in this country.

As our meal was ending, I said to my mother, "That was very satisfying." And she said to me in return, "Yes, it was." I then sat for a moment with the physical sense of being satisfied and with the kind of blank but complete feeling state that was a part of the experience. I was satisfied. I wanted nothing else to eat or drink. I had had just enough, not too much, not too little. I had left nothing in my bowl, nor had my mom. We each had consumed everything that was brought to us: each shred of carrot, each lettuce leaf, nothing wasted.

I then asked Mom how often she was aware of that feeling or experience of being satisfied; how often did it happen to her? She thought for a moment and guessed that one or more times a day, but that she didn't know for sure. And I began to think about that. How often do I experience that kind of simple satisfaction without recognizing it or noting it but merely taking it for granted? Even though it really is a pleasant state, perhaps we often bypass such satisfaction because it's an uncomplicated experience, one that requires nothing else and one that is quite plain rather than richly embellished. At the level of our everyday lives, satisfaction may be too banal a pleasantness to register often in our awareness. We are programmed for more exciting sensations, for louder pleasures.

Yet, Rachel Naomi Remen's account of her mother's last words to her alerts us to the potential power of noticing and bringing more awareness to these gentler traces of happiness. Remen's mother, at age 84, was about to undergo cardiac bypass surgery; she was given only a 40% chance of surviving the procedure.

Remen writes:

Pulling me close, [my mother] kissed me and whispered, "No matter what happens here, I want you to know that I am satisfied". Then she smiled her charming, rakish smile, and they took her away.

As it happened, her mother did not survive the operation. Remen, reflecting on these last words, doubted that it was her mother's considerable accomplishments in life that had given her such ease and contentment in the face of near-certain death. Rather, she says her mother had left her with an important question: How do I live so I, too, might find a deep satisfaction at the end?

Perhaps, then, satisfaction is both simple and deep. As at lunch with my mother, there are those ordinary moments of noticing 'just rightness,' a fleeting harmony of things, a temporary sense of well-being.

And beyond that, there is this notion of 'enoughness,' of knowing how much of a thing is just right, how much work, how much play, how much stuff; a way of living into the wisdom of discerning between need and greed, between ease and indulgence, between completion and compulsive striving. And what if such discerning wisdom results from accumulating moments of satisfaction so that the more we notice our fleeting contentments, the more we learn about what brings our lives into a deeply satisfying harmony?

(Finnish Proverb: *Happiness is between too much and not enough.*)

Linger And Tarry - And Presence

There are words that seem to have been lost in this fast-paced culture of ours. I've made a list of them, and it includes words like linger and savor, tarry and abide, even loll and dawdle. We don't seem to amble or mosey anymore. It seems to be all about time. How there's never enough of it. Or that it goes so fast. Or it's a waste of time to linger.

But is it?

Zen teacher, John Tarrant, writes:

Not doing, having no urgent plans, we dawdle in the intimate while, like a child jumping puddles on the way home from school. The world comes to us then, and we belong in it....At last, we are at home in this fleeting world...

I had a taste of this 'dawdling in the intimate' when my husband and I were preparing to move from the house we lived in for 18 years. Early on, the moving process seemed a little like a life review. Wedding presents from 46 years ago emerged (Who gave us these?), photographs of young people (us) discovered in shoe boxes, high school memorabilia in dusty attic trunks.

As I sorted and culled, I found myself frequently captivated by memories, traveling back to the girl I had been or visiting with friends no longer here. For a while, I gave myself the gift of time, allowing reflection and recalling special moments. I lingered with letters I had received decades before. Sometimes, I spent an entire afternoon with the contents of just one family room cabinet. And though not all of the memories were sweet, I found hints of my own growth and personal journey as I compared where I am now with the person I recalled being then. All of this while staying present to the array of emotions and sensations that accompanied these recollections. I was both remembering and being present in the here-and-now facets of the memory.

As the date of the move approached, however, my relationship with time changed; time became squeezed...or I did. I began to hurry through the sorting, and the letting go. And, as I did, the moving process was reduced simply to hard work. A sense of feeling cramped and tight replaced the looseness and the allowing that had characterized the experience before. In a short while I reached the point where I felt out of space internally. I had no more energy, no more capacity for reminiscence, and no room for the sadness at leaving this home that I loved. At one point, I said to a friend, "I am nearing overwhelment." Fortunately for me, this state did not last long, nor did it tip into the unmanageable.

But the lesson I learned was in the contrast between the lingering and the hurrying. Between the experience of a pace that arose from within me and the pace that felt externally imposed. Between the natural expression of brief tears as I said goodbye to the view of the meadow versus the tightness of my jaw as I bypassed my sadness when I realized I would not see the maples we had planted turn color in the fall.

And I was reminded of how our view of time changes our experience. Episcopalian priest Cynthia Bourgeault writes:

> *I find that the deepest threat on the spiritual path is any sense of urgency of 'I have to have...' or 'I need"... When this urgency enters your life, the rest is going to be correspondingly distorted...*

We lose clarity, we lose our natural, organic processing of experience, and we lose the present moment whenever we are rushing forward toward an endpoint.

Of course, there will be periods in our lives when deadlines approach and when time is limited. But just as that is true, so is it also true that there will be opportunities for lingering and dawdling. Recognizing those opportunities and savoring them all depends on whether we value those slow moments, whether we believe there might be a richness in them, whether we want 'to be at home in this fleeting life.

Brother David Steindl-Rast.

Gratitude

It's not as if any one of us is unfamiliar with gratitude. If asked, we could each make a list of things in our life, probably of things that have already happened today, for which we are grateful: a soft bed, a life partner who makes my coffee in the morning, our furry friends. Grateful that it's so easy to make such a list.

But do we do it?

And it's not as though any one of us is ungrateful.

One writer spoke of a "gratitude ratio" and raised the following questions: Do you experience the good things in your life in true proportion to the bad things? How much complaining do you do versus how much gratitude do you feel? And is that an accurate reflection of how things really are?

I discovered that that ratio is a pretty tricky thing to calculate. Just yesterday, as I was thinking about this, gratitude being on my mind, I had a phone call that ended with my being quite annoyed. Now, the thing about annoyance is that it's often not just one thought that then disappears. Annoyance can last a while - - and I ended up spending a lot of time on that negative side of the ledger. Whereas, when you experience gratitude, it seems as if it's briefer; it doesn't take over your thoughts, or I don't allow it to take them over in the way that annoyance or anger can. So, the positive side of that ledger can really be out of balance in terms of time spent, not just thoughts spent.

There are essentially two energies of the heart, of our inner life: an energy that is contracting and constricting that goes along with impatience, irritation, resistance, anger (we all know what it feels like) and an energy that is opening and expansive that goes along with kindness, generosity, compassion. Gratitude is one of those expansive energies of the heart, one that softens the heart and opens us to contact the other energies of our kindness and compassion.

But when the balance of our ledger that tracks our gratitude ratio is weighted toward the negative, we would be operating more of the time with a constricted and closed heart. Something to contemplate.

I think of that minister who, a few years ago, challenged his congregation to wear purple bracelets to remind them NOT to complain and how difficult his parishioners said that practice was. And Thich Nhat Hanh's 'What's NOT wrong' practice, asking "What's not wrong at this moment...and this one...and this one...?"

Each of these is a practice that reminds us that there is much in our lives to be grateful for, each a practice to help us remember to add to the positive side of our ledger.

<u>Be Glad Your Nose Is On Your Face</u>

Be glad your nose is on your face,
not pasted on some other place,
for if it were where it is not,
you might dislike your nose a lot.
Imagine if your precious nose
were sandwiched in between your toes,
that clearly would not be a treat,
for you'd be forced to smell your feet.
Your nose would be a source of dread

were it attached atop your head,
it soon would drive you to despair,
forever tickled by your hair.
Within your ear, your nose would be
an absolute catastrophe,
for when you were obliged to sneeze,
your brain would rattle from the breeze.
Your nose, instead, through thick and thin,
remains between your eyes and chin,
not pasted on some other place--
be glad your nose is on your face!

Jack Perlutsky

Poetry And Mindfulness

You may have noticed that there is a lot of poetry in this book. I have on my computer a collection of more than 500 poems. How many more, I no longer know. Each of them was chosen for a reason. Sometimes, a line may have captured my attention, like Mary Oliver's *"You do not have to be good,"* or sometimes, I come across a phrase that deserves contemplation, like Stanley Kunitz's *"Live in the layers, not on the litter."* Maybe I sensed a truth that I needed to hear, such as Rumi's *"Patience with small detail makes perfect a large work, like the universe."* Or, I was given as a caution for a day that was to include unpleasant circumstances: *"There's no use hiding it / What's inside always leaks outside,"* by Yunus Emre.

When discouraged by my personal shortcomings, I can find empathy (*Each time you judge yourself, you break your own heart.*Bapuji), humor (*You are a divine elephant with amnesia/trying to live in an ant hole.* Hafiz), solace in my common humanity (*Remember that you are all people and that all people are you.* Joy Harjo) or a reality check (*In this short Life that only lasts an hour/How much - how little - is within our power.* Emily Dickinson)

This collection began to grow when I came to know how useful poetry can be when talking about mindfulness. Several of my meditation teachers quoted verse when giving dharma talks and, to me, the message of the talk was often deepened and made more memorable by the poem. There is something about the careful languaging of a poem - - its brevity or its realness - - that partners well with the principles of mindfulness. So, whether about the importance of slowing down enough to be present (*Efficiency is not God's highest goal for your life,/neither is busyness.* Rob Bell) or being with the difficult aspects of life (*Don't turn your head. / Keep looking at the bandaged place.* Rumi) or acknowledging how our minds are constantly buzzing and grasping (*Everyone is overridden by thoughts; /that's why they have so much heartache and sorrow.* Rumi), poetry has a way to say it.

Of course, there is much more to poetry than a single line or a moving phrase. There is the sound and the rhythm of the words, the patterns and shape of the lines, and the unfolding in successive phrases *"of necessary human information that cannot be communicated in any other way."*(Edward Hirsch, <u>How to Read a Poem</u>)

Consider these stanzas:

later that night
i held an atlas in my lap
ran my fingers across the whole world
and whispered
where does it hurt?
it answered
everywhere
everywhere
everywhere
       Warsan Shire

Can't you see it? A person, sitting by lamplight, a large volume in her lap, tracing a map of the world, whispering to the world as a living thing. And as we engage with these words, we experience the rhythm of the repetition, the insistence of the italics, and maybe, as I do when reading this, especially out loud, feel a welling of compassion for all of those wounded places. Human information, indeed.

As in Warsan Shire's stanzas, poetry often inspires me to practice what is most important in this life.

stop asking: Am I good enough?
Ask only
am I showing up
with love?
       Julia Fehrenbacher

And, in this category of remembering what's important, I have to include Toyohiko Kagawa's singular *Prayer: May I never Yawn at Life*.

With 500 poems to choose from, I could go on and on, citing beautiful, meaningful, funny treasures from my collection. Those I've offered here are samples of words that have somehow spoken to me. I want to say they are words that have entered me. That's how I know they are meant to be guidance on my path. And, of course, what is meaningful can change over time. So I'll include one last selection that has relevance to me at this stage of my life.

> *I pause in this moment*
> *at the beginning of my old age*
> *and I say a prayer of gratitude for getting to this evening*
> *a prayer for being here today, now, alive*
> *in this life, in this evening, under this sky.*
>
> David Budbill

The real voyage of discovery consists of not in seeking new landscapes but in having new eyes
Marcel Proust

Summer Vacation

The pictures on my iPhone from my summer vacation do not include spectacular views of the Grand Canyon or the Eiffel Tower. No Machu Pichu or glamorous islands, either. Instead, what I saw as I reviewed the images was a tree that was more than 100 years old, one that I saw each day as I walked through the city park with my dog, magnificent in size and nobility. I also see a weather front marching toward me: a wall of pinkish-grey fog, still miles away across the bay, blocking the spit of land behind it. Another image is that of the most intensely vivid rainbow I had ever seen, its arc reaching high in the sky and extending beyond the eye of the camera lens. Not exactly the items on many bucket lists or the stuff of "1,000 Things to Do Before I Die."

There is the view these days that accumulating experiences is the route to happiness; this view asserts that accumulating things, as our consumerist culture urges us to do, offers more ephemeral pleasures than the memories we can revisit again and again of the places we've been and what we did in those places. But it seems to me in order for that to be true for experience collectors, and, therefore, to count in the happiness formula, there has to be genuine contact with an experience. What I mean by that is that the place, the sight, and the activity have to touch us in a visceral way; we have to be open and receptive to its impact so that we feel as well as see what is present so that we participate as well as observe. Without an elemental, physical ingredient to integrate us with an experience, that experience becomes no more than a place we can say we visited or a sight we witnessed; been there, done that, saw it.

I recently saw a picture of the crowd gathered before the Mona Lisa at the Louvre. Instead of gazing at the painting, many in the crowd are too far away to see any details; instead, they are holding their smartphones above their heads, taking a picture of the painting. Is that 'seeing' the Mona Lisa? Or what about the mobs in Venice or on the Spanish Steps in Rome?

While travel can widen our perspective on many aspects of life, it doesn't guarantee that we will see and take in these opportunities deeply enough to be enriched by them.

The gift of mindfulness practice is that we can become so much more attuned to the experiences we have every day that our quotidian lives have that same richness, that same potential for happiness that exploring a foreign country can bring. That I have taken pictures of my summer experiences does enhance the memories of those experiences: standing beneath that magnificent tree in the park induced awe and wonder that something so strong and massive could emerge from a tiny seed. Watching that weather front approach for nearly an hour, Carl Sandburg's 'catfeet' came alive. And that rainbow - - being with its full cycle of appearing and then gently vanishing on the same day that my son's dear dog had passed away - - made the 'rainbow bridge' a truth. Each with its own felt sense in the body.

I suppose this is what a vacation can offer us: the time to be more present in our experience, as well as the time to learn how enriching being present can be. Then we can take home not only the memories that being fully present embeds in our brains, but we can bring into our everyday lives a strengthened practice for collecting 'experiences' in our own backyard.

If we are honest, and if we look back at the past with an impartial eye, it's clear that most of the fundamental circumstances that order our lives are out of our hands. We don't pick our parents. We don't choose our bodies, our talents, our temperaments or most of the other seminal elements that determine our fates . . . What we do choose, especially as we increase in wisdom and years, is the way we approach the circumstances of our lives.
Harry R. Moody

With mindfulness of mental states, we can choose whether we practice peace or go to war, whether we want to be imprisoned and stuck or to release the painful states and be healthy. We can learn to release those mental states that bring us sorrow and foster those states that bring us joy.
  Jack Kornfield

CHOICES: Outlook and Attitude

  Outlook

  What Are You Baking?

  Everything Is Amazing And Nobody's Happy

  Agency

  Beginner's Mind

  Not Knowing

  The Peace Of Being

  Acceptance

  Attention And Observation

  Mom And Scrabble

  Making Room For Possibilities

  Refuge

Outlook

The fact of the matter is that, in this human embodiment, we are hard-wired with a negativity bias - - and that bias is not our fault. It comes with the territory of the more primitive part of our brain that is neurologically prepared to look for threats and dangers. Because of that wiring, a negative event is registered faster and more automatically than a positive one; positive events require more time to be stored.

Not only that, some of us are genetically predisposed to have more vigilant or melancholic dispositions; some of us were raised in families where pessimistic or critical attitudes prevailed. We had no control over these factors either.

So, choosing options that are in our own best interest and lead to more positive outcomes may not be automatic or easy. But while this negativity bias and/or these other conditions over which we had no control may not be our fault, as humans, we are also wired for the capacity to bring awareness to our internal experiences and to cultivate more positive ways of managing these influences.

It is not at all surprising that research has shown that an important ingredient of well-being is this very choice that we make of how to view our world. Regardless of how that view is oriented at this moment, we can alter it in the next and, importantly, we can alter the direction of how the brain itself tilts. Certain areas of our brain are activated when subjects report a sense of well-being. Richard Davidson's brain imaging studies have found that if we take in the positive more consciously and notice the goodness in ourselves and others, we not only will have a greater sense of well-being but those areas of the brain increase in brain matter. In fact, just 7 hours of loving kindness or compassion practice over a two-week period results in changing the brain in that direction.

It makes sense, then, that paying attention to our outlook can make a difference in how we incline ourselves in and toward the world. Yes, mindfulness practices ask us to deal with and not bypass the hard things. They will occur in every life. But so do joyous and often unseen or unnoticed pleasures. We can adopt a perspective and a set of attitudes that enable our vision to take in and savor moments that are beautiful, enlivening, joyous, and uplifting. In fact, this is necessary so that we don't lose the capacity for appreciation, for pleasure, for awe.

Poet Jack Gilbert argues.

"We must have the stubbornness to accept our gladness in the ruthless furnace of this world."

<u>A Brief For The Defense</u>

*Sorrow everywhere. Slaughter everywhere. If babies
are not starving someplace, they are starving
somewhere else. With flies in their nostrils.
But we enjoy our lives because that's what God wants.
Otherwise the mornings before summer dawn would not
be made so fine. The Bengal tiger would not
be fashioned so miraculously well. The poor women
at the fountain are laughing together between
the suffering they have known and the awfulness
in their future, smiling and laughing while somebody
in the village is very sick. There is laughter
every day in the terrible streets of Calcutta,
and the women laugh in the cages of Bombay.
If we deny our happiness, resist our satisfaction,
we lessen the importance of their deprivation.
We must risk delight. We can do without pleasure,
but not delight. Not enjoyment. We must have
the stubbornness to accept our gladness in the ruthless
furnace of this world. To make injustice the only
measure of our attention is to praise the Devil.
If the locomotive of the Lord runs us down,
we should give thanks that the end had magnitude.
We must admit there will be music despite everything.
We stand at the prow again of a small ship
anchored late at night in the tiny port
looking over to the sleeping island: the waterfront
is three shuttered cafes and one naked light burning.
To hear the faint sound of oars in the silence as a rowboat
comes slowly out and then goes back is truly worth
all the years of sorrow that are to come.*

What Are You Baking?

Some 40+ years ago, I was a graduate student in the clinical psychology program at Virginia Commonwealth University (VCU). When I look back on that training and the field of psychology in general, as it was then, in comparison to what is happening in psychology now, the differences are huge. Perhaps most significant for the aspiring clinician that I was then, the view of the humans we were to be 'treating' was strongly biased toward finding out what was wrong with them so we could decide on the appropriate interventions. What disorder did they have? In fact, Martin Seligman, a well-known American psychologist, has remarked that

> *for the last 50 years of the 20th century, professional psychology ought better to have been called victimology, so obsessed had it been with the study of what's wrong with people--what's wrong with their emotional lives, their relationships, their physical brains, and why they fail and feel bad and do terrible things to each other.*

No wonder going to a therapist was considered stigmatizing by so many people.

Of course, today, there is still a substantial focus, as there should be, given to easing the suffering of serious mental conditions, but it is notable that the past 20 years have seen the academic world giving significant attention to re-balancing this view. Much of the credit for this shift has gone to Seligman because of the challenge he issued to the field of psychology when he assumed the presidency of the American Psychological Association in 1998. First, he claimed that it was important to recognize that psychology was half-baked. He said, "literally half-baked. We have baked the part about mental illness [but] the other side's unbaked, the side of strength, the side of what we're good at." He went on to say:

> *This is because, since World War II, psychology has concentrated on repairing damage within a disease model of human functioning... Psychology's focus on the negative has left us knowing too little about the many instances of growth, mastery, drive, and character building that can develop out of painful life events.*

For 50 years, psychology apparently had its own negativity bias. Fortunately, academic psychology seemed to take Seligman's challenge to "bake the other side" seriously. The trend in the field in the 21st century has been toward the scientific study of what makes people happy and good. Seligman himself went on to found The Positive Psychology Center at the University of Pennsylvania, which, by the way, as of this writing has about 37,000 people enrolled in an on-line introductory course about positive psychology. University of North Carolina's Barbara Fredrickson offers a free Intro to the Science of Happiness on her website.

So, why is this notable?

First, it's good news that we humans are no longer only studied as flawed beings to be fixed; rather we are also seen as beings with innate capacities to love, to care, to connect, and to work for the common good.

Second, though I have not seen this connection made elsewhere, I believe that mindfulness, in general and Jon Kabat-Zinn, in particular, played a major role in tilting psychology in this positive direction. From 1979 on, when formulating and teaching Mindfulness-Based Stress Reduction (MBSR) at Massachusetts General Hospital, patients participating in Kabat-Zinn's program were told," From our point of view, as long as you are breathing, there is more right with you than wrong with you…"

He went on to write: The practice of mindfulness involves finding, recognizing, and making use of that in us which is already okay, already beautiful, already whole by virtue of our being human...

So by the time Seligman issued his challenge in 1998, MBSR and mindfulness had been in the air for almost 20 years, baking the other side.

The mindfulness view of who we are allows us to acknowledge our less than skillful, sometimes dysfunctional tendencies arising from our judging minds, our threat-sensitive brains, and our personal reactivity while at the same time assuring us that who we are is also so much more.

As an experiment, It might be interesting to check in with yourself from time to time to find out how evenly you are baked to reflect as you go through your day or week: where does the dial land when your thoughts are about you? Toward the dissatisfactions you have about this self of yours? Or toward the positives, the goodness that is particular to you? And where does that dial land when you think about other people in your life- or other people in general? How much critical commentary do you find? How much goodness is registered?

In other words, what are you baking?

Everything Is Amazing and Nobody's Happy

This is the title of a comedy bit that CK, a comedian, delivered on Conan O'Brien's show. CK was mocking how spoiled we all have become. A little piece of his bit went like this:

"People come back from flights, and they tell you their story: "They made us sit on the runway for 40 minutes.' ...Oh, really? What happened next? Did you FLY through THE AIR, incredibly, like a bird? Did you partake in the miracle of human flight? You were sitting in a chair, IN THE SKY?"

CK was pointing out how much we take for granted, how we don't even see these modern miracles.

The truth is, though, most of us would complain, at least to ourselves, if we were stuck on the runway for 40 minutes. Or if we lost our luggage. Or maybe even if they ran out of our favorite beverage. These are all examples of how much we want things to be the way WE want them: convenient, as advertised, and comfortable. And when they are not the way we want them to be, we complain, we get agitated, we suffer, and we then try to fix things more to our liking.

Zen teacher Ezra Bayda has said that we can never underestimate our desire to be comfortable. Take a moment to think about that: we can never underestimate our desire to be comfortable. He sounds a bit like Pema Chodron here when Chodron likens our ego to wanting "a room of your own, a room with a view, with the temperature and the smells and the music that you like. You want it your own way."

Our egos, our desire for comfort, and our resources for creating our comforts all can cocoon us to those kinds of wonders that CK was talking about. We don't even notice them anymore because we are so busy complaining and thinking about how we want the world to suit us and then doing what we can to rearrange things so that it does. Our culture conditions us to move away from that which is merely uncomfortable,

But James Baraz, a meditation teacher in California, takes a different angle on this subject of complaining. He created the "Awakening Joy" program now in its 20th year. He tells the story of his 89-year-old mother, Selma. Selma was a complainer and a worrier who admitted to her son that her lifetime habit of seeing a glass half empty left her so accustomed to focusing on what was going wrong that she had trouble connecting to the gratitude for the many things in her life that were going right. So James, being a good son, devised a gratitude practice for his mother. He suggested to her that each time she complained about something, she added the phrase "and my life is very blessed." So, when Selma said, "My TV isn't working right" she followed with, "And my life is very blessed." Or, "My daughter hasn't called in two days---and my life is very blessed." Over a period of time, this practice apparently resulted in her mood growing brighter; even his sister commented after a few weeks, "What did you do to Mom?" Seven months after beginning this practice and on the occasion of James' birthday, Selma sent her son this poem:

> *Ninety is just fine with me, I no longer rant and rave*
> *About where the world is heading and my exclusive job to save.*
> *I wallow in contentment and know that I am blessed*
> *Awakening to the joy of living at its best.*
> *I'm happier than I've ever been and truly mean each word.*
> *The thoughts that caused the worries now all seem so absurd.*
> *Though my eyesight has been dimmed I see clearer than before,*
> *The glass is not half empty, it's overflowing to be sure.*

Selma had a mind habit, a practice, if you will, of seeing a half-empty glass, and this habit clouded her seeing. Mind habits in particular and habits in general, along with comfort-seeking, mask our experience of the moment.; and can lead to missing moments of wonder. So, while gratitude practices are a way of reminding ourselves that, indeed, we are fortunate to be comfortable, I am also thinking here not so much of remembering to be thankful as noticing what is here right now, which is remarkable. Selma said she sees more clearly than before. This has to do with what we turn towards, what we keep in front of us, and what we incline our minds to see and be with. And what we are most open to. This whole notion of all the wonders that go by unnoticed was underscored

when I came across a wonder-full poem that just grabbed me and wouldn't
leave.

<u>If the moon came out only once a month</u>

If the moon came out only once a month
people would appreciate it more. They'd mark it
in their datebooks, take a walk by moonlight, notice
how their bedroom window framed its silver smile.

And if the moon came out just once a year,
it would be a holiday, with tinsel streamers
tied to lampposts, stores closing early
so no one has to work on lunar eve,
travelers rushing to get home by moon-night,
celebrations with champagne and cheese.
Folks would stay awake 'til dawn
to watch it turn transparent and slowly fade away.

And if the moon came out randomly,
the world would be on wide alert, never knowing
when it might appear, spotters scanning empty skies,
weathermen on TV giving odds - - "a 10% chance
of moon tonight" - - and when it suddenly began to rise,
everyone would cry "the moon is out," crowds
would fill the streets, jostling and pointing,
night events would be canceled,
moon-closure signs posted on the doors.

And if the moon rose but once a century,
ascending luminous and lush on a long-awaited night,
all humans on the planet would gather
in huddled, whispering groups
to stare in awe, dazzled by its brilliance,
enchanted by its spell. Years later,
they would tell their children, "Yes, I saw it once.
Maybe you will live to see it too."

But the moon is always with us,
an old familiar face, like the mantel clock,
so no one pays it much attention.

Tonight why not go outside and gaze up in wonder,
as if you'd never seen it before,
as if it were a miracle,

What would it be like if we were to see 'as if we'd never seen before?' Or perhaps asking ourselves the mindfulness question (paraphrasing teacher Jonathon Faust): What is between me and seeing as if I have never seen before?

Meditation and mindfulness practices offer us 'skillful means' for becoming less 'spoiled' or more wonder-filled.

In formal sitting meditation, we can begin to see ourselves more clearly: how our minds work, how we cloud our immediate moment with thoughts, stories, distractions and attempts to control our experience rather than actually experience it. Meditation can help us unhook from the mind habits, like Selma's habit of seeing the glass 1/2 empty, that cloud our seeing clearly. When we sit in silence, allowing our minds to settle with a breath practice and then welcoming whatever arises in the moment, we begin to notice the patterns of our thoughts, the beliefs about ourselves that are buried beneath our self-talk. And we can learn to see through them; see through them not only to our inherent goodness but to see through them to what is actually in front of us in this moment. And be reminded that everything is amazing!

Or, we can imitate Mary Oliver. This is her prose poem titled.

<u>Foolishness? No, it's not</u>

*Sometimes I spend all day trying to count
the leaves on a single tree. To do this I
have to climb branch by branch and
write down the numbers in a little book.
So I suppose, from their point of view,
it's reasonable that my friends say: what
foolishness! She's got her head in the clouds
again.*

*But it's not. Of course, I have to give up,
but by then I'm half crazy with the wonder
of it - - the abundance of the leaves, the
quietness of the branches, the hopelessness*

of my effort. And I am in that delicious
and important place, roaring with laughter,
full of earth praise.
                    Mary Oliver

May you see more full glasses, more full moons, and more abundance of
leaves!

The range of what we think and do
is limited by what we fail to notice.
And because we fail to notice
there is little we can do
to change
until we notice
how failing to notice
shapes our thoughts and deeds.

R.D. Laing

Agency

We are living in a time of disquiet when there isn't much stability to point to, and it often seems as if there isn't much we can do about any of what's going on in our world. Those external events over which we have no control impinge on our collective well-being and diminish the sense of agency in our lives.

The word agency, as I use it here, is a concept that social scientists define as the capacity of individuals to act independently and to make free choices. Having a sense of agency refers to the human capability to influence the course of events in our lives through our actions. Most of us want to believe that we have the power to effect changes to make an impact by our actions; unless people believe they can produce desired effects by their actions, there is little incentive to act or to persevere in the face of difficulties. None of us likes the opposite of that belief in our effectiveness. Those opposites, like helplessness or feelings of futility, create the ground for the adverse mental health consequences that seem to be so prevalent in Western cultures.

Richard Davidson, founder of The Center for Healthy Minds at the University of Wisconsin and pioneer researcher in the effects of meditation on our brains, specifies two critical ingredients for our sense of well-being that are familiar to mindfulness practitioners. And these are two capacities that offer us the possibility of agency in our lives. The first of these two is attention. He suggests that we have choices and can make a difference in our sense of well-being by being intentional about how we direct our attention. For example, I know that if I watch a horror movie, I will have nightmares. If I look at funny dog videos, I smile and feel warmth. What I pay attention to, what I input into my system, has an effect on my state of being. And this is true for all of us. And there's never been a more important time to monitor that input because our attention is considered a commodity by the electronic media. You can tell that is so just by the pop-up ads that constantly appear on your screens.. Those are bids for our attention. And the more we use those media, the more the ads become targeted to our personal interests, concerns and buying habits. Our attention is wanted, and the attempts to seduce it are crafty. But our attention is a power that is within our control if we are awake and mindful of how we CHOOSE to use it.

In the 1970s, when I was studying psychology in graduate school, an important new area of research ignited the field, one that now seems to be so obvious. Investigators studied the impact that systematic tracking of one's own behavior, called self-monitoring, had on the behavior itself. The behaviors chosen for study were negative ones, such as smoking and overeating, and two significant results emerged. The first was that subjects who tracked those behaviors were often surprised at the frequency in which they engaged in them; second, that just by monitoring them and with no other intervention, the frequency of the behaviors dropped significantly.

The conclusion offered by the researchers? That self-monitoring was a significant tool in effecting behavior change. But as I reflect on these results today, it seems to me the most important aspect of their research had to do with the power of attention and awareness and - - the inverse power of inattention and ignorance.

Paying attention to where your attention is, recalling the standard definition of mindfulness, and paying attention on purpose make a difference.

Mindfulness is purposeful. It is intentional. And we can pay attention on purpose to that which is of benefit to us rather than to that which depletes us. This is not to say that we should ignore the tough stuff that is in the news. We can be informed without being saturated. We can learn to discern our limits by paying attention to our bodies and being intentional about offering ourselves alternative healthy or healing inputs. We can ask ourselves if we spend as much time turning our attention to what nurtures us as we do with those inputs that are unnerving or upsetting. We all differ in the degree to which we are susceptible to the prevailing negativity, AND learning more about our personal limits by paying attention to how inputs affect us emotionally and physically is a mindfulness practice.

We can also bring mindful awareness to the second of those ingredients that contribute to well-being: attitudes we have toward our experiences. This aspect of mindfulness concerns how we are disposed to meet the more daily experiences of our lives. In this moment, are we irritated or patient, curious or bored, kind or mean-spirited? It turns out that the challenge of mindfulness practice is not simply to be aware of things, to notice, but to do so with a particular attitude or tone: one that is receptive, accepting, curious, respectful and nonjudgmental. Kabat-Zinn says that such attitudes are a way of directing and channeling our energies so that they can be most effectively brought to bear in the work of growing and healing and, in this way, contribute to our well-being. It is asking ourselves the question: How am I reacting to this moment, this experience? How are my energies directed?

Mary Oliver offers an example: She writes

If I walk out into the world in irritation or
self-centeredness, the birds scatter.

On the other hand, do we incline ourselves, like Mary Oliver, towards

...the pleasure that fills you
as the sun
reaches out,
as it warms you
as you stand there,
empty-handed

With the practice of paying attention to our inner states, we can make more discerning and nurturing choices about directing our attention and attitudes. We can access our agency at the moment.

Beginner's Mind

A famous Zen story tells of a university professor who travels to Japan to learn about Zen. There, he meets with a Zen master. As the master quietly prepares tea, the professor is talking about Zen. The master pours the tea as the professor talks, filling the visitor's cup to the brim and then continues to pour. Tea spills out of the cup and onto the table. The professor, watching the cup overflowing, could no longer restrain himself.

"Stop pouring," the professor shouted. "The cup is full. No more will go in."

The master looked at the professor and said, "You are like this cup. You are full of your own opinions and speculations. How can you learn about Zen unless you can first empty your cup?"

And this, of course, illustrates the equally famous quote from Zen master Shunryo Suzuki:

"In the beginner's mind, there are many possibilities, but in the expert's, there are few."

The beginner's mind, then, is empty of preconceived ideas, ready to accept new input, open to all possibilities and free to doubt. In other words, there has to be room in the mind for something new.

Our energy is constantly being snapped up by ideas, concepts, thoughts, emotions and other mental objects that are a screen between ourselves and reality. The paradox is that to become more conscious and more aware, one must KNOW less; that is, let go or move beyond the thoughts and concepts that already populate the mind in order to make room for the new news.

Wisdom from the Talmud reminds us that "We do not see things as they are; we see things as we are ." This speaks to the notion that each of us has a unique set of lenses for making sense of our experience. So, I made an inventory of my lenses the perspectives through which I see my world.

I am female. I am of a certain age and generation. (Think of the difference this makes just in terms of how I see technology, for example.) I am a privileged white person. I am educated, I have a unique family history, and I am an American. I am a grandmother. And these are just the obvious lenses through which I interpret and view the world.

On top of these acquired and personal lenses is the fact that our brains are what one scientist described as "talented forgers." Our brains fill in gaps for us without us even knowing it. They are high-speed computers that often get things wrong - - and even more often distort what is right in front of us.

Andrew Newberg, a neurotheologist at the University of Pennsylvania, wrote that.

> *Having an accurate perception of reality is not one of the brain's strong points....the human brain seems to have difficulty separating fantasies from facts. It sees things that are not there, and it sometimes doesn't see things that are there.... the human brain selects a handful of cues and then fills in the rest with conjecture, fantasy, and belief.*

That's one problem that makes the attitude of a beginner's mind difficult. Another is that we become immune to the miracles of the familiar. We bypass the simple wonders of the world on our way to our important lives. I think of the White Rabbit in Alice in Wonderland-- "I'm late, I'm late, for a very important date!" And the lines that Emily speaks in Thornton Wilder's <u>Our Town</u> after she dies and looks at those still on earth as reminders of how much we take for granted.

Goodbye
> *to clocks ticking*
> *and food*
> *and coffee*
> *and sleepin'*
> *and waking up*

Oh Earth
> *You're too wonderful*
> *for anybody*
> *to Realize you!*

Routines and sameness and on-our-wayness numb us to what is really in front of us.

Plus, we like certainty a lot. It gives us a sense of control over the unknown. But what do we really know for sure? Especially about what's next or about what's really true. I like what Suzuki Rochi said about this. He said,

Not knowing does not mean you don't know. Not knowing means not being limited by what we know, holding what we know lightly and being ready for it to be different. Maybe things are this way. But maybe they are not.

The advice from Rochi, then, is to take ourselves and what we know less seriously. And from Newberg, the advice is to remember that our brains make mistakes. And this further advice :

Everyone thinks he knows what a lettuce looks like. But start to draw one and you realize the anomaly of having lived with lettuces all your life but never having seen one, never having seen the semi-translucent leaves curling in their own lettuce way, never having noticed what makes a lettuce a lettuce rather than a curly kale...What applies to lettuce, applies equally to the all-too-familiar faces of husbands...wives...
Frederick Franck

A mind is like a parachute. It doesn't work if it's not open.
Frank Zappa

Not Knowing

A couple of interesting research findings to share:

Given the choice between waiting for a lesser amount of pain and instantly receiving a greater amount of pain, people chose the latter. Researchers concluded that we want to get things over with. Instead of staying in the present moment and being with some uncertainty as to what and when the experience of pain would occur, subjects had to move things along.

Brain imaging shows that our brains feel rewarded when we make a choice - - ANY choice. In other words, just the act of making a decision, without regard to its quality, pleases our neural circuits, lighting up the same pathways as other pleasures like winning a game.

Just as other studies have found that research subjects don't like sitting with their thoughts, these kinds of findings imply that we seek completion, that we prefer doing something rather than having gaps in activity.

As I was thinking about this, I was reminded of my docent training at the Virginia Museum of Fine Arts (VMFA). I learned then how little time people spend with a work of art. One survey found that the average viewer goes up to a painting, looks at it for fewer than two seconds, reads the wall text for another 10 seconds, glances at the painting to verify something in the text, and moves on. Another survey concluded that people viewed the art for a median time of 17 seconds. The Louvre reports that people looked at the Mona Lisa for an average of 15 seconds, which makes one wonder how long they spent on the lesser-known works in the collection.

What do you suppose happens in that 15 or 17 seconds? In general, I can speculate that it may be coming to a 'decision' about that painting or sculpture: I like it or I don't like it. Getting the 'hit of a decision' and then moving on. As a docent, one of the main emphases in training had to do with how to engage the viewers with the art, how to move visitors through that initial reaction of liking or not liking or simply 'now I've seen it' into a deeper experience of the work. The strategies I learned to use were similar to the practices of the 'Don't

Know' mind: arouse curiosity to explore an experience and use Inquiry to go beyond what is already known or obvious.

The art of Not Knowing has to do with bringing an open mind to our experiences. We humans tend not only to want quick decisions, fixes and solutions, as those researchers found, but we also don't like empty spaces or gaps. We have an urge to close the gap of openness. We tend to fill silence and at least 50% of our moments with mind chatter, with a narrative stream of stories, judgments, of self-referential preferences - - none of which leaves much room for new ways of looking or learning to enter. The practice of Not Knowing asks us to engage with what is real in this moment, with a receptive quality of mind, with a willingness to consider possibilities and to relinquish our preference for certainty and allow for discovery.

We learn through meditation practice that we add to what is happening at the moment with our thinking, and we find how difficult it is to come back to the actual experience we're having at the moment. Don't Know mind, not knowing, is like a simple breath meditation practice. When we place our attention on the sensations of the breath instead of what we're thinking about, being with what it's actually like, in that moment and the next, that's practicing don't know mind.

Why do it?

For one thing, we can have richer, deeper experiences as with the example of looking at an object of art. Moving past prejudgments and personal preferences to a broader outlook can expand the present moment to include what we otherwise would miss. We can notice and observe other dimensions of the moment other than the ones we are already familiar with.

And we can bring this attitude into our relationships. I am very familiar with the tendency to fill in the blanks with my assumptions of how my husband might think about something or even be certain that I know what he might say next in a conversation. A Don't Know disposition in a relationship is one that allows the other to be just as they are, without anticipating or expecting the next thing, without guessing or assuming that you know what is in their heart or head

- - even after 50+ years. Psychologist Ronald Siegel suggests the following practice that he titles Three Objects of Awareness.

When talking with another person, bring your attention to:

1. Your body sensations, thoughts and feelings

2. Your partner's words, body language, and facial expression

3. You felt a sense of connection and disconnection with your partner.

By attending to the felt sense of connection or disconnection, along with your inner emotions and those of the partner, richness is added to the relationship. It's a way to approach a conversation with more curiosity and with the intention to see the other more clearly. And it's a way of taking in the experience of being with someone rather than filling in, which tends to be all about ourselves.

Really, the bottom line of Not Knowing practice counteracts our tendency to rely so heavily on what we already know in favor of meeting the moment with presence, curiosity and inquiry.

Suzuki Roshi said,

Not knowing does not mean you don't know. It doesn't require that we forget everything we have known or to suspend all interpretations of a situation. Not knowing means not being limited by what we know, holding what we know lightly; we are ready for it to be different. Maybe things are this way, maybe they are not.

The Peace Of Being

I wrote this in August during one of our summers in Maine. For the previous five years, my husband and I had rented a cottage in a small mid-coastal town on Penobscot Bay. What had begun for us as a search for respite from the Southern heat had evolved into something much more, something we did not know we wanted or needed. We did not come to hike, though we had done some of that. We did not go there to kayak or sail as many do, though we had done that, too. In fact, for us it wasn't really a vacation spot anymore as it was at first. We continued spending time there so that we would remember what it was to be.

Our days were spent quietly. They were long. The sun rose early that far east; by 5:30 a.m., our curtainless aerie of a bedroom was flooded with the intense first light. We breakfasted on the deck overlooking the glistening harbor, and, likely, one of us chose a random card from a deck of Tao verses to read for our daily contemplation. What followed was never planned until it happened: maybe a long walk to the city park (estab. 1908) still with its original metal playground slide and swing-set beckoning to Belfast's children, or, in the other direction, strolling into town past the bright household gardens, evidence of green thumbs everywhere, to amble down brick-fronted streets into the bakery for a fresh Maine blueberry scone. Often, though, the morning simply unfolded into the afternoon on that deck. Reading, raising the binoculars to spy on one more boat as it left or arrived in port. Waiting until low tide to step down to the beach, touching toe into cold water or just changing the seat of reverie to a massive boulder bared by the ebbing tide. There was nothing to do, nowhere to go except to move in the direction that the moment called us towards. Settling into a natural rhythm, our bodies had forgotten.

Joseph Campbell wrote:

You must have a room or a certain hour of the day when you do not know what was in the morning paper, when you don't know who your friends are, you don't know what you owe anybody or what they owe you - but a place where you can simply experience and bring forth what you are, and what you might be.. At first you may find nothing's happening...But if you have a sacred place and use it...something will happen...

Acceptance is about the relationship we have with what arises- our thoughts, feelings, sensations. It is the willingness of the heart to be with what's here and it has to do with our relationship to/with reality. How do you meet what is true?

Acceptance

One noted teacher has said, "In any situation in life, confronted by an outer threat or opportunity, you can notice yourself responding inwardly in one of two ways. Either you will brace, harden, and resist, or you will soften, open and yield." And isn't that true? Can't you tell within yourself almost immediately how you respond to some event, say an invitation to a party? Your response might be: I want to do this (open to it), or I don't want to do this (resistance), or you may be conflicted. Even then, you have a sense of your disposition or attitude toward the event, even if it's mixed.

There's a kind of continuum between the two extremes of acceptance and resistance.

At any given moment, we fall somewhere on that continuum of being fully open to and receptive of what's happened to us and within us - - the acceptance end of the continuum - - or we find ourselves being at odds with our reality, denying, avoiding or wishing things were otherwise, the resistance end of the continuum. And, though it may be difficult to recognize and to exercise, we do have some choice about where on that continuum we find ourselves.

As I've reflected on times in my life when I have been especially aware of this acceptance/resistance continuum within me, the examples that came to mind have shown up in the bigger moments of life, like during the experience of cancer and while being the primary caretaker of my mother as she neared the end of her life. By the time each of those difficult situations occurred in my life, my practice was far along enough to have inclined me toward a willingness to be full with my experience, to accept the reality of the circumstances and the reality of what was happening within me, to let it touch me, and to stay there long enough to come to some clarity about the best actions to take.

But as I reflected further, I also thought of an experience that occurred when my practice wasn't established enough to do that. Years ago, a good friend had done something that hurt me, and it wasn't the first time something like this had happened to her. Rather than be with the feelings this aroused in me, the anger as well as the woundedness in my heart, I reacted to an old story that had immediately appeared. My thoughts went directly to she doesn't care about me, my feelings don't count, I don't count. Instead of staying with my hurt, allowing it to touch me, I chose to believe the story of her indifference that I fabricated. Over the next few days, the story repeated itself many times, and eventually, I walked away from this friendship without saying anything to her, ignoring her calls. I guess it's called ghosting now. A petty response that wasn't worthy of me or fair to her.

I've come to realize two critical things from this reflection. First is the awareness that, in each case, the conditioning I had experienced in my family was a part of those moments, appearing pretty much right away; the old stories rush in first. Being with my mother, for example, the story was that I 'thought' I was supposed to be 'strong,' 'dutiful,' and 'uncomplaining.' Whatever I was feeling shouldn't matter, even though I was, in fact, tired, grieving, and worried. Once I was willing to acknowledge that I was in a very difficult, emotionally wrenching situation, once I allowed myself to see the reality of my experience, I was able to give myself a time-out, some space that then allowed me to come to some clarity about what I needed and what my mother needed. The second realization: not until I respected my emotional and physical truth was I able to 'see' how I wanted to be and what I wanted to do.

With my friend, if I had looked beyond my automatic reaction, I might have been able to discern that she was careless, not uncaring; I may have been able to recall the times that were proof that she valued our relationship. Plus, I may have realized that I would have best been served by telling her how her behavior had impacted me, owning and respecting my feelings with out blaming her for them. Instead, I lost a friendship of many years that still leaves me feeling sad when I think about it.

Acceptance does not mean approval. I didn't have to approve of what my friend did. Nor did I have to approve of my feelings. The feelings were real; my interpretation of the event may not have been. Acceptance simply means recognizing the urge to walk away and the feelings beneath that urge, allowing their presence and then considering what, if anything, to do about it.

In the context of a mindfulness practice then, acceptance is really about being with the truth of your experience, not someone else's version of it. I needed to be willing to look at what else was beneath my inclination to hear those old voices. Someone said acceptance requires engagement with what is. Yes, it does. It requires saying Yes to what is there.

But, it takes significant strength and motivation to let go of how you think things should be or how you wish things (or others) were in order to work with your reality, especially when you don't like it. Ultimately, though, acceptance can create the space, emotionally and cognitively, to explore alternatives more clearly. And it has seemed to me that each time I have done that, it is an act of self-compassion -to admit to my reality, to own it and allow it.

Actually, that's the third realization that I had as I sat with this. It is compassionate to acknowledge what is yours instead of somehow diminishing it, ignoring it or assuming you can't handle it. We carry so much conditioning around with us, it is always a factor in our experience. But it does not always tell us the truth about our experience or our situation. How we feel is real, but emotions may be aroused by remnants from our history that distort our perception of the moment. If we respect what we feel enough to look more deeply into it, to engage with it, to allow it to be there, we have a chance to see whether the old story is a part of the present moment.

Of course, there are situations we cannot live with. No one should accept physical or emotional abuse or believe that they deserve mistreatment. The mistreatment itself is a reality that needs to be acknowledged; it is a story that needs to be seen beyond.

And finally, acceptance is not about behavior. It is not what you do. Acceptance is what happens before you choose to act. It's a beginning; It's what leads us to possibilities and to choices.

Teacher Jonathan Foust offers his students this question: What is between me and acceptance of this moment? Often, the answer has to do with what we are telling ourselves or an old story that no longer has relevance in this circumstance. But sitting with that question can help clear the way to your authentic experience of the moment so that an opening can be found to move skillfully forward.

Mary Oliver

Attention And Observation

Scientists contend that the age of smartphones has left us with such a short attention span even a goldfish can hold a thought for longer than we can. Researchers surveyed 2,000 participants in Canada and studied the brain activity of 112 others using electroencephalograms. The results showed the average human attention span has fallen from 12 seconds in 2000, or around the time the mobile revolution began, to eight seconds.

We as human beings have the capacity to place our attention where we want it, to have some control over what we are noticing, over what we are bringing into our conscious awareness at any given moment. When you stop to think about it, this ability to direct our attention is an amazing faculty. And one that has a significant impact on our well-being since how we focus our attention shapes our mood and dictates where we devote our energy. Research studies have found that when our mind wanders into the past or spends too much time in the future, we are more likely to feel depressed or become anxious. Simply stated - - what you pay attention to determines your mind state. And how we walk in this world depends on that state of mind.

In the context of mindfulness, attention is the first quality that meditators begin to practice and cultivate by focusing on the breath and returning attention to the breath when the mind inevitably wanders. This breath practice is the mindfulness training ground of attention. Repeated over time, it strengthens the 'muscle' for staying with the present moment experience. We can train our attention to be more stable, to dwell for longer periods of time on what is beneficial. And as we train our attention and our mind settles, we create more space. But attention requires a willingness to be affected by what we notice, to be impacted by life, by what is, by the way things are.

Poet Mary Oliver's life experience has something to teach us about this. She had suffered a difficult childhood that included trauma and abandonment. "It was a very dark and broken house that I came from." She acknowledges in her poetry, over and over again, that her refuge and much of her healing was due to her relationship with and her sense of belonging to the natural world - - being with and in the family of things. From the time she was very young, her walks into nature became what I believe were frequently repeated acts of self-compassion. She recognized her connection to the life she observed on these walks and, though unflinching in her notice and acceptance of the suffering and pain in the natural world, this noticing did not diminish her experiences of delight and awe. She understood that nature's hardships were a part of the cycle of things, as were the joys. It was as if this understanding allowed her to find room in her own heart to hold not only her own suffering and pain but to accept the pleasures that life had to offer as well. Nature was a spacious container for her.

It is that lens of attention, how she used it, how she refined it, how she trained it, that serves as an example of its power. Her keen focus on these walks took her out of her wandering mind, a mind that she had elsewhere stated was constantly busy and into the present moment. She once described her vocation as "the observation of life," and she learned that observing, looking closely at what was there before her, often opened the way to a sense of wonder and awe.

The capacity that each of us has to place our attention where we want it gives us some control over what we are noticing and over what we are bringing into our conscious awareness at any given moment. In fact, recent research has found that how we focus our attention shapes our mood and dictates where we devote our energy. As Rick Hanson, a neuropsychologist, writes: Whatever we hold in our attention has the power to change our brain. And that matters to our well-being. Somehow, Mary Oliver sensed this.

From <u>Mornings at Blackwater</u>

What I want to say is
that the past is the past
and the present is what your life is,
and you are capable
of choosing what will be darling citizen

While she didn't choose the family or the household into which she was born, she could choose what she brought into her consciousness, where she focused her attention.

For Mary Oliver, becoming the rich lens of attention allowed her to bring a concentrated awareness to the sensate experiences that were available to her in the present moment of those walks she took: the smells, the sounds, the visuals of nature, the very content of her poetry. It's easy to make the leap that those kinds of experiences were a healthy replacement for memories of her past or for the conjuring of self-judgments. In fact, she says as much: Stepping out into the world, into the grass, onto the path, was always a kind of relief. I was not escaping anything. I was returning to the arena of delight. (p.151, Upstream)

In one of her poems, Mary offered three rules for How to Live a Life. The first of these is: Pay attention. The second: Be astonished. And the third: Tell about it. But without rule number one, Pay Attention, she couldn't have had the experience of astonishment, of delight, of the good stuff. "Shining the light of clear sustained attention" led to everything else.

Mom And Scrabble

When my mother was living in an assisted living residence, I would often have dinner with her there. Dinner was a big deal for the residents since being able to get to the dining room signaled to everyone something about their physical and mental condition: well enough to navigate the hallways and elevator and sharp enough to engage in the interactions that were bound to happen.

On one such night, we were seated at a table strategically placed in the center of the room for maximum visibility and reserved for those with a guest. Its location invited a stream of residents to stop by. First, there was Fay, the one that no one particularly liked because she complained all the time. During this visit, though, she was kind to me, asking after my son's family, then lingering with her questions (did you enjoy the meal? Where did you say you lived?) as long as she could. Soon after, Mom's good friend Miller greeted me with an invitation to play bridge; the always elegant Miller; I complimented her on her bright blue blouse and pretty necklace. Erwin came by next to tell me to be sure to look at the photograph she had taken of my mother ("It's a really, really good one") and added that her sacroiliac was causing her a lot of pain. Then a man approached us whom I had never met; Mom later said that he makes the rounds each night, stopping at every table just to say hello. As I said, dinner is a big deal there.

And with each visitor, I became more and more aware of how much a new presence means to these residents. These are not the most forgotten elderly among us; these were all individuals who had enough money to live quite comfortably to receive the basic attention of staff regarding their physical needs; they were well-nourished and entertained. But in a fundamental way, they may nevertheless have felt forgotten. I became aware of how much Fay, Miller and Erwin simply wanted to be seen, to be noticed - - as a person, as a human being, not so different from me, only a bit older.

Though I had intended to eat and run, I simply couldn't leave my mother after these encounters and after watching her closely during the meal. She enjoyed so much the attention our table was receiving; she, too, had the human need to be acknowledged, to be seen.

So, I asked her if she would like to play Scrabble after dinner. Her "Yes" was a happy one. We went to her apartment and set up the game. Mentally, I checked the clock (it was only 6:30), but I had wanted to leave before dark, and I had been looking forward to an evening all by myself since my husband was out of town, watching one of my favorite recorded shows with a glass of wine; nestling in bed to finish the good book I had been reading. Usually, Scrabble with my Mom took a good while. Her competitive streak was still very much alive; she pondered every play at length, even when her score was far behind mine. She never tossed in her tiles early. And her physical difficulties at that point lengthened the game. Her hands were so inflexible that she struggled with the tiles, and her tremors made it even more difficult to handle those small pieces and place them on the board. I knew better than to help her, though. She preferred to do it herself. And then there was the slow calculation of the value of her word. Again, I didn't offer to do it for her. Somehow, we both knew that her ability to do this simple math was an unspoken measure of her independence. But that night, a new hindrance to a speedy game appeared.

At this point, I should tell you that patience is not a virtue of mine. In fact, it is a practice edge. My mother had commented on this before, that I am not good at waiting in line for appointments at traffic lights; you get the picture. When we played Scrabble at my house, I dealt with the intervals between my plays and hers by looking at magazines, reading articles, and thumbing through catalogs, but at her apartment, none of these diversions was available to me. Already, having glanced at the clock was all it took; I had been moving ahead, pushing time forward.

I was the first to place my word on the board. When my mother began her turn, she was clearly struggling to read the letters she had drawn from the bag. And she was unable to read the words I had spelled on the board. So she picked up the entire board (fortunately, it was one of those that had a separate slot for each tile) and held it close to her face. She studied it and put it down; she then held her tile rack close to her face, picked up the board again and finally was ready to form her word. By the time she placed her word on the board and calculated its value, minutes had gone by, and I knew that I was going to be here quite a while.

Thank goodness for my practice. Thank goodness for mindfulness. Thank goodness I was at least awake enough at that moment to check in with myself. I found that my body was tightening; there was that familiar jaw clenching. And an as-yet-slight agitated restlessness was showing up in my legs. The beginnings of Impatience had arrived. With that recognition, I realized I had a choice at this moment. I asked myself, " How do you want to be with her tonight?" "How do you want to meet this next moment and the next one?" "With a heart closed by impatience"?" or "with a heart that is open to seeing your mother"? I'm sure you know which intention I chose.

My mother was a tough old bird. She had known hardship and loss. And, unlike Fay, she didn't complain. At 94, she had macular degeneration; her vision had deteriorated so significantly in the time since we had last played Scrabble that she had had to develop this new strategy for reading the tiles and the board. She neither made excuses for this development nor allowed it to rush her turn. Over the next two hours, she expressed no exasperation with herself, only frustration that she was drawing all of the worthless "I-s" and none of the more valuable letters from the bag.

So two hours passed. I checked in often with myself. If I noted any rising tension, I simply gazed at my mother's face and breathed in the gift of her aliveness - - allowing the love I felt for her to be in the space between us.

Who won the game? We both did.

Making Room For Possibilities

During the early days of the pandemic, I was talking to my daughter-in-law, who worked for a major healthcare system. Her job then involved overseeing the re-distribution of personnel within the system, which, because of the impact of the Coronavirus, had required drastic shifting. In this work, she had a birds-eye view, a very broad perspective, on how healthcare was being affected by the pandemic. She commented during our conversation that the healthcare system in this country will never be the same again, and that it will be permanently changed by the shifts that have been required during this upheaval. We didn't talk about what those changes would be or how things would be different, just that it would be dramatic. But it was in hearing that I began to hold the notion that out of the chaos, the unknown consequences, the shared collective experience that will leave no one untouched, this huge, dynamic upheaval we were all a part of held possibilities that we cannot yet know.

And I asked myself: what if that attitude of possibility translated into my mindfulness practice? What would that look like? In other words, what could I shift in my practice to make room for possibility, for what might be new?

And just like seeing red cars all over the place when you are thinking about buying one, there were other inspirations supporting this attitude of curiosity and openness. I remember seeing the pictures of the sky in Delhi, India before the city was on lockdown and then later pictures taken during the lockdown. Really dramatic, the before: a brown fog that blurred buildings and people; one could almost feel the particulates in the air; and the later: a clear blue sky that had some commenting with amazement at how beautiful the sky is. It had been so long since they had seen it.

There is something reassuring about the clarity that comes when things stop, are halted, seeing what is there behind the debris; there are also other pictures of uncrowded tourist sites and empty streets, that space that is created when there is a pause in our usual activities.

Poet David Whyte described it this way: "It's as if the world was given a rest so we could see what it's like when we leave it alone. And what we see is fresher, healthier, more beautiful, quieter." In a way, this echoes an interesting project created by artist Scott Polac titled "Applause Encouraged." This took place at Carrillo National Monument, a beautiful rocky outcropping on the Pacific coast in San Diego. On a cliff overlooking the ocean, forty-five minutes before sunset, a greeter checked guests into an area of foldout seats formally cordoned off with red rope. The guests were ushered to their seats, asked to turn off their phones and were reminded not to take photos. They watched the sunset, and when the sun had completed its descent, they applauded. Refreshments were served afterward.

Polac had designed a set of conditions that held open a contemplative space against the pressures of habit (not checking on our phones), familiarity (oh yeah, another sunset), and distraction (chatting with your neighbor), pressures that constantly threaten to close off that space. Doesn't that sound a bit like where we were when quarantined? Our usual pressures of habit - - the time we wake up, our morning routines, driving to work - - were up for grabs. Or they could have been. Many of the things we do mindlessly, without thought or attention, were upended, leaving us asking ourselves: what do I do now or instead? And, as with the guests at sunset, offering opportunities to take in more fully what is right there in front of us without distractions.

That includes our internal experiences. So, my practice begins now with the intention to be curious and open, to allow for a space inside me that doesn't get filled right away. The poet, Jane Hirshfield, knows this space.

She writes:

...you aren't doing anything but offering up your attention, yet, somehow, doing nothing allows mind, body, emotion, the rain on the roof to come together and reveal themselves. It's as if you were to sit very quietly in the woods; after a while the animals begin to emerge, and you see the full amplitude of life that is in fact, already there.

Hirshfield's words were literally validated when it was reported that after only 4 weeks of closing Yosemite, the wildlife had begun to come out of hiding. This 'making room,' 'opening to,' and waiting are ingredients of an intentional process, one of emptying and letting go, one that creates an internal space for new or as yet unknown possibilities from within to arise. Perhaps this is one mindfulness lesson we can take from the pandemic: what might emerge if we create more space for our inner fog to lift? more silence for the full amplitude of life within to arise?

<u>The Peace of Wild Things</u>

When despair for the world grows in me
and I wake in the night at the least sound
in fear of what my life and my children's lives may be,
I go and lie down where the wood drake
rests in his beauty on the water, and the great heron feeds.
I come into the peace of wild things
who do not tax their lives with forethought
of grief. I come into the presence of still water.
And I feel above me the day-blind stars
waiting with their light. For a time
I rest in the grace of the world, and am free.

Wendell Berry

Refuge

Though first appearing in print in 1968, Wendell Berry might have written this poem yesterday. He speaks directly to our growing despair for the world as each day seems to bring more news of pain and suffering among us. While it is true that mindfulness practices ask us to find the courage to deal with the difficult challenges we face in life and that the practice of turning toward what is hard strengthens our muscles for coping with the unexpected, sometimes we need to give ourselves a break as Berry did. When his despair became too great, he found a place of rest and peace "into the presence of still water." Sometimes, we need to give ourselves permission just to rest, just to be, just to feel safe. Sometimes, we need a refuge. A place where we can release the heaviness we are bearing, a place where we let go of trying to make anything better, a time when we can put on pause our care-taking of others. We need our practice to help us find that still water. To settle us.

Our practice can bring us back into a more harmonious balance with ourselves. A refuge allows us to let go of effort and simply sit with what we already know how to do: to be with our breath. We don't have to perform. A refuge helps us find peace and balance in the midst of the upheavals in the external world.

Refuges can take many forms. For me now, it is my cushion. And sometimes the rocking chair on my front porch. I have friends who find gardening to be calming. And that is a kind of measure for a refuge: somewhere that offers spaciousness for being. Spaciousness can mean time, it can mean quiet, it can mean room; time enough, quiet enough, room enough to hold all that needs to be put down for a while. One of the first refuges I discovered as a child (though I didn't call it that then) was a tree or, rather, in a tree. When my family visited my grandparents, and I wanted some relief from the small house and the too many adults, I would climb an apple tree that grew nearby. The tree was well-sited for contemplation because it was on top of a hill that overlooked a long sloping meadow ending at the edge of a forest valley that stretched into the distance. While I wasn't exactly meditating in the tree, I was alone with my thoughts and my daydreaming, in the quiet, with the natural world all around me.

During the pandemic, many of us needed shelter from the virus. We needed to stay home and away from most people. We needed shelter from the carelessness and insensibility of others who had chosen to ignore the precautions that were suggested. Now, we continue to need refuge from the bombardment of information that we receive online, on social media, and on TV. We need refuge from the other (no matter how wonderful) beings who share our living space. We also need shelter from ourselves, from the business of our minds, from the strain of adjusting to whatever the new normal is and how that new normal is constantly changing.

A refuge is a means, an option, for helping to bring us back into a more harmonious balance with ourselves. It's an opportunity for letting go, releasing any heaviness, relieving or setting aside the burdens for a while. It offers a chance to re-align, recover harmony within, to re-member ourselves.

And the world cannot be discovered by a journey of miles,
no matter how long,
but only by a spiritual journey,
a journey of one inch,
very arduous and humbling and joyful,
by which we arrive at the ground at our feet,
and learn to be at home.
                    Wendell Berry

DEEPENING: Wisdom, Interconnectedness and an Open Heart

WISDOM

What If?

To me, the "What If" questions posed by the poem are an invitation, one that invites us to meet our everyday happenings with attitudes of reverence, respect, and wonder - - whether in our relationships, our conversations, or our being in nature. In a sense, that is a definition of the sacred. It introduces the dimension of the spiritual into what each of us comes across in our lives. What if our religion was each other? Or what if our words were as thoughtful as prayers?

The wisdom that gave birth to mindfulness holds that we, as human beings, have far more potential for goodness and wisdom than we know. And from a mindfulness perspective we are always potentially becoming more than we already are or perhaps revealing more of what we already are.

When we quiet our mind in meditation, we create a doorway into the stillness and depth in the heart space. We can then find that spacious presence of our natural awareness that has room for all of our experiences as well as room for the possibilities of wisdom and compassion. We may even find our belonging there in the commonalities of the human condition. From a sense of connectedness, it becomes possible to leave behind, however temporarily, what poet Mary Oliver has called the "egocentric insistence on separateness."

That is the "more than," the space that transforms our vision of who we are and what the world is.

Mary Oliver put it this way:

I would say that there exist a thousand unbreakable links between each of us and everything else, and that our dignity and our chances are one. The farthest star and the mud at our feet are a family; and there is no decency or sense in honoring one thing, or a few things and then closing the list.
The pine tree, the leopard, the Platte River, and ourselves - we are at risk together, or we are on our way to a sustainable world together.
We are each other's destiny.

Wisdom and Love are the two great wings of Dharma. Whether we are in the swirl of a busy life or in the deep, still silence of retreat, a clear mind and an open heart are the paramount forces we cultivate as both the means and the end of our path.
Joseph Goldstein

Wisdom

In the Tibetan Buddhist tradition, the bodhisattva of wisdom is Manjushri, sometimes depicted as an elegant figure sitting in tranquil meditation upon a ferocious-looking wild beast. In this version, he holds a sword in his right hand to cut through all of the obscurations that interfere with the clear-seeing capacity of wisdom; in his left hand, he holds a scroll that represents 'prajna' - - or that ability to penetrate into the heart of the matter (the truth of how things are). The definition of wisdom in this tradition, Manjushri's essence, is just that: seeing into the heart of things without the influences of self-concern or personal conditioning getting in the way. Manjushri himself represents our 'inner Buddha:' the wisdom capacity within each of us.

That he sits on the back of a wild beast, in meditation, signifies his composure even in the most dire circumstances; he has 'tamed' his wildness, his reactivity; he can keep his animal nature in check but, at the same time, the shadow side - - this tendency to reactivity, to instinctual protectiveness - - is present right there for all to see. He hides nothing; he is living the reality of life.

This image of wisdom speaks to our very human nature. It is the recognition that we all have these reactive tendencies within us: to want things that aren't good for us, to avoid things that are difficult, to react with anger or impatience; all of those aspects of our human nature that come with having a primitive brain still protecting us as well as the conditioning that we learned in our families and our culture. At the same time, Manjushri's calm presence tells us that there is the possibility of managing those tendencies so that they don't get us into trouble or take us away from accessing our own wisdom, from seeing clearly how things are.

The Buddha had a simple test for measuring wisdom. You are wise, he said, to the extent, you can get yourself to do things you don't like doing but that you know will result in happiness, and you are wise to the extent that you refrain from doing things you like but know will result in pain and harm. What he seemed to be pointing out was that to act wisely, wisdom has to outwit our shortsighted preferences, those moments when our 'humanness is asserting itself.' And that wisdom is the infrastructure of our choices. The manifestation of wisdom, then, is in the choices we make about how we live.

This view of wisdom seems very down to earth. It asks us to investigate or pay attention to the results of what we do of the actions we take. We learn what tendencies leave us feeling small, disliking ourselves, or regretting something; we become more aware of what brings us pleasure or satisfaction. We can then make some choices: can we refrain from those behaviors that are harmful to ourselves or others, and can we engage in those that promote our well-being and the well-being of others?

From this perspective, wisdom develops as we assess our own behaviors with honesty and with an intention to live according to what matters most to us. It is a 'gradual training, an organic unfolding' according to teacher Jill Shepard. To me, this recognizes both the fact that wisdom requires time as well as some resolve to cultivate. Typically, we view life through the veils of our collective histories, through the veils of our conditioning, through the unquestioned beliefs that we carry, and through the preferences and expectations that we have. This is another way of saying that we see things as we are, not as they are.

In fact, it may not be possible for any of us to see 100% of the time without these misconstruing brains convincing us that things are one way versus another. But we can become aware that we have these biases, these veils. Rather than being an intellectual pursuit, cultivating wisdom occurs as we pay attention to and learn from the internal and external consequences that we experience in our own lives. Meditation and mindfulness practices expose these inclinations, and by cultivating space, there is room for discernment and choice.

With that awareness, we can wield Manjushri's sword to cut through the beliefs and habits that veil our clear seeing and interfere with our wisdom.

From this perspective, Wisdom for me has become a do-able pursuit. It is a collective kind of growth that happens over time; it has depended on intention, awareness, recognition as well and self-forgiveness for the un-wise moments. And, while far from the finish line, over time, as I have allowed myself to open more, to release thoughts, to trust in the space that is more empty than full, unexpected understandings of 'how things are' have arisen. I have been offered glimpses of 'the more than.'

Surrender

It was New Year's Eve, and I was in a meditation hall with 70 others in the middle of a five-day silent retreat. The fall had been a jolting one; my father-in-law had died that September, I had just a few weeks before completed an 8-day intensive program structured to enable the 'letting go' of emotionally constricting patterns carried forward from childhood, and our much beloved 13-year-old pet had died in our arms just three days earlier. I was at the time of this New Year wide open and tender - - and feeling very ready for some quiet, settling silence.

It seemed, though, as if the silence was not to be settling at all. During most of the sits so far, the third day into the retreat, I was aware of the same old thoughts and small mind; my meditations felt superficial and mostly boring. And here I was again in a sit, another head struggle going on, aware of wanting this site to be different and also aware that this was directly counter to being with whatever 'is' in the moment. In my frustration, I decided to become curious to ask myself, "What is stopping me from going into my experience more deeply?" "What is getting in the way?"

That inquiry allowed an image to form; I saw a scene, an outdoor scene with a path and trees. But the setting looked artificial, like a child's wooden town set with wooden trees and a wooden path. No life there. Disappointed, still frustrated, I entered the scene in my imagination and walked a little way on the path, but only found myself becoming impatient, then disgusted. Still, in my imagination, I walked up to those trees neatly lining the path and shoved them, pushing them down. They toppled - - those fake-looking trees; they just fell away, and I climbed over them, went behind them, past them onto the hill beyond.

As I climbed the hill, I could literally smell the earth, very real, and a sadness came over me at that moment. I thought of Andy, our sweet dog, and I began to cry. Memories of the other wonderful dogs who had been our companions; all were gone. Tears flowed, and tightness gripped my jaw and throat. Then, my father-in-law - - gone. In the meditation hall, now fully present to my experience, thoughts of My Mom, now 90, who had lost a husband, brothers, a sister and all of her life-long friends, and how much grief she has endured through these losses. I thought of my son and his wife and the pain they will feel for their children and for the losses they will experience.

Then, a huge weight of dread arose and a fear that something had happened to someone I loved. I literally felt pulled from my cushion; someone needed me. Something tragic had happened. Shortly (thankfully), the meditation bell sounded, and I left for my room, where I immediately, breaking the commitment to silence, called my mother, my husband and my son. All was well with them - - but I was not. My dread was gone, my fear for them was gone, but my aching, my deep sorrow remained.

I sat in the chair in the room and asked myself if I wanted to stay with what was happening to me. This was unfamiliar and strange and arising from a source I didn't recognize. Can I do this? Am I willing to allow the full power of what was welling within me to surface? I was by this time sobbing from my wide-open heart, loving so much, so much to lose. I wanted to cry out to my loved ones, "Stop right where you are. Don't move or change or grow up until I love you. Give you so much love that I haven't any left." How can I love deeply and hold the hurt that love brings? Can I do this? And then the dread arose again, and fear came into my heart, the deep knowing that life was like this for me, that I would suffer loss and for each and every one in my life, that they too would suffer loss. And that all beings everywhere, anyone who loved, would suffer the pain of loss.

I knew I could choose to stop this, to go outside or even leave the retreat; I also knew that I couldn't leave, that this was the point of being here, of being in this life at this moment.

It was then that I surrendered to the moment, to the sorrow, to the fulness of what was happening. Time passed; I experienced more waves of grief and sadness. With each welling of emotion, I felt yet another extension into the natural order of things. In that time, my sense of the world and of life shifted. I had understood before, in the rational part of my mind, that death and grief and loss were universal, that they would visit me and everyone I loved; this understanding now became lodged in my heart, and there, waiting, was a depth of compassion and a sense of unity with all beings in that compassion. I was becoming aware viscerally of the common human condition and in that awareness of the nature that is within all of our hearts, to love and to know the pain of loss and the deep compassion that is available through that pain.

My words for this experience are inadequate. I can say that I had fallen into the stream of life and was led to a place of the Bigger Story. Once I yielded fully to what was happening, I had no sense of where this was leading; I let go into the unknown. In the end, by being present to those powerful waves, I came to the truth of compassion: to the truth that in the experience of my grief, I was connected with every other being. Though I had read this in a book, I now knew it in the deepest way: that if we can be present in our grief, great compassion arises. It is there, within us and under us, and is a part of our True Nature.

You mustn't be frightened
if a sadness
rises in front of you,
larger than any you have ever seen;
if an anxiety,
like light and cloud-shadows,
moves over your hands and over
everything you do.
You must realize that something is happening to you,
that life has not forgotten you,
that it holds you in its hand
and will not let you fall.
Rilke

The work becomes that of making an accurate inlet of the heart without closing off to the feelings of others or to the depth of things that are ours to feel...the fiber of the one heart we are given is strong and light enough...to bring us to the wind that is whispering.....Let down, let go, the world will carry you.
Mark Nepo

Impermanence And Grace

In the spring of the year that my father-in-law turned 88, I asked him what piece of wisdom he would pass on to those of us younger than he. His reply:

Life is dynamic. It never stands still. It is always changing. And there are two kinds of change: evolutionary and sudden. Sudden or catastrophic change can not be ignored but with evolutionary change, we are not always aware that it is happening as it happens until something brings it into focus. Without this awareness of more subtle changes, you miss a great part of what life is about: its innuendos.

He went on to say

"It isn't what happens to you that matters. What does matter is how you take it. That matters much, and it matters long."

I was struck that his words so closely paralleled the Buddhist notion of impermanence. How often have you said to yourself, "I wish this could last forever." Or "I wish I could freeze this moment." Knowing full well that with the next breath, everything might dissolve or shift. We want our joys, like the feeling of euphoria when my newborn son was placed on my belly or the sense that "all's right with the world," to last. But that is not the nature of joy. As my father-in-law pointed out, life is dynamic; it doesn't stand still. What counts, "what matters much and matters long," is how we relate to those joys, those moments. If we hold to them tightly, we suffer as they inevitably slip away. If we constantly replay them in our memories, living in the past, then we miss the life that is present now.

The same inevitability applies to times of difficulty. Though sadness may seem to linger longer than joy, it, too, will slip away if it is allowed to leave. But again, despite our suffering, we may prolong our grief or our anger or our anxiety by dwelling in those mind-states, by wishing things were different or by attempting to deny their existence at all. Those strategies do not allow the release, the moving through and beyond the pain. They may postpone it for a time, but they do not remove it. If we spend our energies trying to change that which cannot be changed, we miss the nuances, the innuendos, and the richness of all that is in this present moment.

My father-in-law's wisdom was simple: Be with what is. You might think that it was an easy life that allowed him to be so equanimous and so accepting of change. But that had not been his fate. He nursed and then lost his first wife, the mother of his children, to cancer. He then nursed and lost his second wife to cancer. He had undergone not one but two multiple bypass operations and had lived for the last few years on about 15% of his cardiac capacity. He had yielded to "what is" many times; with each change in life conditions, he learned to re-group, to adjust his sense of what life now had to offer him and to move on to explore the possibilities of his new circumstances. Over time, his capacity for graceful accommodation burgeoned to the point that his resilience and 'noble flexibility of being' became exemplars to each of us in his family.

My father-in-law, HD as we called him, died in September of his 88th year. His heart had continued to weaken, and it was on a Thursday that his hospice nurse told him and his wife that he was in the final stages of heart failure and that he had no more than a few days. HD asked what would happen once the dobutamine pump that had been stimulating his heart for months was removed. He was told that his death would follow within hours. HD and his wife and son then thought about those next few days. They planned a celebration to take place at home following his memorial service; HD dictated the menu for that celebration. On Thursday and Friday, family members were called and began to arrive. Those who couldn't travel talked with HD on the phone; to each, he gave a loving goodbye: to a niece, he said that he had always admired her energy for life; to a grandson leaving the next day for Iraq, he said this would be the last time they would talk and that he was proud to be his grandfather. Lastly, the final resolve: HD and his wife decided that the pump should be removed at 6:00 pm Saturday so that all who were on their way to see him would have arrived.

By Friday night, a vigil had begun: wife, sons, step-children, and grandchildren bound together with love for this man who was leaving us.

Around dinner time, HD asked to get out of bed so that he could be a part of the gathering in the living room. His sons lifted him into a wheelchair and guided him to a place where he could see everyone and where everyone could hear him. With a gin martini in hand - - a treat he had not allowed himself for at least a year because of his medications - - HD waved off fussing over his appearance. Despite his bed-head hair, disheveled pajamas, the oxygen and dobutamine tubes hanging from his body, and his thin chest peeking out from his open robe, he was a dignified presence. Upright in that chair. Holding our gazes. His bearing, his being emanated his willing surrender to what was soon to happen; to us sitting around him, we saw no visible fear of what awaited. It was as if he wanted to leave us as we had always known him: enjoying conversation, enjoying the energy of people, enjoying the moment right where he was. And it was as if he were saying a thank you to us for being with him, for all that we had meant to his life. He then held court for an hour or so telling amusing stories to his grandchildren about his college days. His composure, his acceptance, his 'being with,' his final gift to them and to us. And ours to him: our laughter and loving gaze to be among the last perceptions that he experienced.

After the 'party,' HD told his wife, in the privacy of their bedroom, that their original plan would have to change. Six o'clock tomorrow, he said, was too far away. It would have to be sooner. Since the last grandchild was to arrive around noon, he asked that the pump be removed at noon. Then he went to sleep, and he did not wake again. And so it was. At noon on Saturday, with all of us at his side and with a prayer, the nurse removed the pump. HD died two hours later, within a circle of held hands and grieving hearts.

Catholic friends have said that HD died a "holy death."

What I have come to see is that HD's 'holy death' was simply a continuation of his practice during life: by over and over meeting and accommodating the truths that life presented, he could meet the truth of his death without struggle and with the light of his spirit intact, still giving and glowing until it left his body.

Seeing with eyes of wholeness means recognizing that nothing occurs in isolation... Seeing in   this way, we can perceive the intrinsic web of interconnectedness underlying our experience and merge with it. Seeing in this way is healing. It helps us to acknowledge the ways in which we are extraordinary and miraculous, without losing sight of the ways in which we are simultaneously nothing special, just part of a larger whole unfolding, waves on the sea, rising up and falling back in brief moments we call life spans.

Jon Kabat-Zinn

Interconnection

Mary Oliver's delight in the world's beauty was hard-won. Her work often invites readers, by way of her own example, to gaze upon their grief, despair, and loneliness, but she does not belabor those aspects. Instead, her words encourage readers to turn toward something larger. This shift in focus from an intimate, personal experience to the interconnected movements of the wider world appears throughout her work in a way that seems both elemental and mystical.

Once, years ago, I emerged from the woods in the early morning at the end of a walk and - - it was the most casual of moments - - as I stepped from under the trees into the mild, pouring-down sunlight, I experienced a sudden impact, a seizure of happiness. It was not the drowning sort of happiness but rather the floating sort. I made no struggle toward it; it was given. Time seemed to vanish. Urgency vanished. Any important difference between myself and all other things vanished. I knew that I belonged to the world and felt comfortably my own containment within the totality...As I say, it was the most casual of moments, not mystical as the word is usually meant, for there was no vision or anything extraordinary at all, but only a sudden awareness of the citizenry of all things within one world: leaves, dust, thrushes and finches, men and women. And yet, it was a. moment I have never forgotten and upon which I have based many decisions in the years since.

The poet calls us " to our belonging in the family of things" in 'Wild Geese.' This sense of herself as a part of the family of things, as part of the natural flow of life, appears over and over again in her work. After eating fish,

"Now the sea is in me: I and the fish, the fish glitters in me; we are risen, tangled together, certain to fall back to the sea." With this sense of connectedness, she gives herself over to her sensate "animal body" and leaves behind, however temporarily, "egocentric insistence on separateness."

This notion of our interconnectedness, our commonality with all living things and our dependence on each other for survival certainly had been highlighted by the Covid pandemic; we have seen the frightening lesson of how easily a virus is transmitted from one human to another and how rapidly it spread over the globe. Clearly, we are not isolated. We have been vividly exposed to our shared vulnerabilities, our human vulnerabilities.

When Oliver describes an experience she had in the woods where "any important difference between myself and all other things vanished" and then the lines in another poem: "we are at risk together,… we are each other's destiny," she also indirectly makes clear the necessity for treating all other beings, including the earth, with compassion; for if our destinies are intertwined, to harm one living thing, is to harm all living things. She is saying we Inter-are

<u>The Moth, The Mountains, The Rivers</u>

*Who can guess the luna's sadness who lives so
briefly? Who can guess the impatience of stone
longing to be ground down, to be part again of
something livelier? Who can imagine in what
heaviness the rivers remember their original
clarity?
Strange questions, yet I have spent worthwhile
time with them. And I suggest them to you also,
that your spirit grow in curiosity, that your life
be richer than it is, that you bow to the earth as
you feel how it actually is, that we - so clever, and
ambitious, and selfish, and unrestrained - are only
one design of the moving, the vivacious many.*
Mary Oliver

202

Faith

At the time of this story, my friend Jill, 63, a cancer survivor, was recovering from recent knee surgery. In other words, she was not in peak (or maybe even reliable) physical condition. She had retired from her lucrative career as a consultant to Silicon Valley high-tech companies with the intention of being a doting grandmother and community volunteer. Consistent with this intention, she attended a meeting of non-profit organizations in need of highly skilled professionals willing to work in an unpaid capacity. It was at this meeting that she heard of an overseas group searching for someone with her skill set to help an African non-profit youth AIDS agency in Uganda. Despite her age and health concerns, she volunteered for a 12-week assignment to guide this agency toward becoming more effective in its delivery of services.

It was with excitement and understandable trepidation that Jill undertook this work. She became a regular and articulate journal keeper via e-mail from the moment of her arrival in the country. Her story, as it unfolded, was astonishing in many respects, but as her time with the agency lengthened, she found herself questioning the leap of faith that took her there. She had encountered deception, corruption, manipulation, failure and helplessness, not to mention the poverty and abuse she saw all around her. She experienced the limits of her competence in effecting change - - and this is a brilliant woman. She became angry and nearly spent. Yet her correspondence continued to be inspiring. Over time, she came to understand that this particular journey was not about 'doing good' in Africa; instead, it really had been about her coming to terms with herself, with her expectations, with her hidden assumptions, with her shadow, with the very sense of whom she saw herself to be.

So, what has Jill's story to do with faith?

Perhaps it is a Western notion that we should be able to 'see' the results of our actions, that if we work hard enough, competently enough and with 'good' intentions, there will be an identifiable effect. And I'm not talking about personal satisfaction or reward here; just evidence of an impact. But, if the universe is constituted of an interconnected web, we cannot possibly know how our actions will reverberate. Whether on ourselves or on external circumstances. There is left only the trust, some would say faith, that when we act in concert with our own most deeply felt truth the outcomes will have meaning for us and/or others at some point in the future.

This, for me then, is a partial answer to what and in whom I can place my faith. I can place my faith in the belief that, for my friend, the combination of her gifts and her experiences will bear a fruit about which nothing is yet known. And I have faith because I believe that.

> *It is not given to us to know which acts or by whom will cause the critical mass to tip toward enduring good. What is needed for dramatic change is an accumulation of acts, adding to, adding more, continuing...*
> Clarissa Pinkola Estes

And, ultimately, I can place my faith in the human spirit, in Jill's, in my own, in the immanent goodness that is at the core of every being.

> *So, despite troubling politics and despite personal challenges - - No matter what we encounter in life, it is faith that enables us to try again, to trust again, to love again. Even in times of immense suffering, it is faith that enables us to relate to the present moment in such a way that we can go on we can move forward, instead of becoming lost in resignation or despair. Faith links our present-day experience, whether wonderful or terrible, to the underlying pulls of life itself.*
> Sharon Salzberg

Awakening Our Hearts

This is the true story often told by meditation teachers of an 800-year-old Buddhist sculpture commissioned by monks and placed in a temple in a monastery in Thailand sometime in the 13th century. It is a huge statue of the Buddha, almost 10 feet tall. As reconstruction work occurred in Thailand over the centuries, entire monasteries had to be moved, and for 20 years, this Buddha was housed under a tin-roofed shed because there was no temple in the vicinity large enough for it. Finally, in 1954, a new monastery and temple were constructed that could house this sculpture. At the time, the huge figure was covered in a coating of stucco and plaster, painted gold and inlaid with pieces of colored glass. It was not considered especially attractive, but its size was commanding, and it had survived for centuries. So it was to be moved. During the attempt to lift the figure from its pedestal to go to its new home, the lifting ropes broke, and the statue fell hard to the ground. And some of the plaster coating cracked and fell off.

One of the workers noticed that a shiny surface had been revealed under the stucco and called the abbot of the monastery. It was discovered as the coating was gradually peeled off that, underneath the coating, this Buddha was solid gold. At 5 1/2 tons, it is thought to be worth more than $250,000,000. It now rests in shining splendor atop a 4-story marble-lined temple in Wat Traimat in Bangkok. The story now told is that the sculpture was covered over by monks in the 18th century as a way to protect it from invading Burmese armies; for more than 200 years, it held the secret of its true value hidden beneath its coarse coating.

In some ways, we are like the golden Buddha. From childhood on, we all have developed some kind of protection to take care of ourselves, whether from family difficulties or perceived inadequacies or vulnerabilities. We all have some constrictions, some closing off of ourselves. These protective strategies served a purpose; they were needed at some time. It is a part of living a life. Practicing mindfulness helps us become aware of how and when, as well as where these protections arise, what we resist, when we withdraw, and what arouses fear or anger. It is the heart practices that help us soften and open those places, loosen our shells so that we can become more fully who we are, more integrated, more in touch with our own goodness.

The Brahmaviharas, the four qualities of an awakened heart, offer us a way to redirect ourselves out of those protective, reactive patterns. Practicing any one of them aims our intentions and attitudes in a different direction; they aim toward opening ourselves to the whole of who we are at our core. In the Buddhist tradition, the attributes of loving-kindness, compassion, appreciative joy and equanimity are already within us. Every one of us. They are relational, connecting us to the deepest parts of ourselves as well as to other beings.

However, it is important to note that these are aspirational and interwoven practices.

They are aspirational because it is a rare being who can abide in any one of these states of the heart all the time. For most of us, we just have moments, and then we fall back into our usual thought patterns and our usual ways of being oblivious, self-focused and attached to our beliefs. But each little moment of awakening to the alternatives matters. Each moment of compassionate action chips away at the covering of our heart; each acknowledgment of joy helps us remember the possibilities that life holds for us and others; each act of kindness wafts love into the air, and each moment of equanimity introduces another instance of peace and calm into the world.

And the Brahmaviharas are Interwoven because practicing any one of them facilitates the cultivation of the others. Repeating loving kindness phrases is a concentration practice that helps develop the stability of the mind that supports equanimity. Practicing Compassion enables the heart to stay open to suffering, strengthening our ability to withstand the winds of change that bring difficult moments of loss and distress; practicing appreciative joy reminds us to keep our hearts open to possibilities and supports the buoyancy of loving kindness.

That's why practicing with these qualities however we choose to do so matters. When these qualities guide our intentions we make a difference in the air around us, in the words or gestures we communicate, in the actions we take. We may never see or know the results of what we carry into the market place but our heart will remember our kindnesses, our compassionate actions, and our joyful moments.

<u>The Scent of Love</u>

As the heart of the wayfarer
turns to the Beloved
So the heart of the world turns.
Silently we each going
The secant of love
Into the marketplace
Of our ordinary lives
Where it touches
The hearts of others.
Unknowingly
those around us
Are awakened
To the joy
that has been missing
Life has been
Without the recent
Of the sacred.
When this returns
To our city streets
It will draw people to the garden
Of their soul
And a deep hunger
Will begin
To be
Satisfied.
          Llewellyn Vaughan-Lee

Loving Kindness

Of the four qualities of the heart, this is the one that received most of the attention in the teachings of the Buddha. It is considered an "indispensable foundation of an awakened heart." The basis of the Brahmavihara of Metta or Loving Kindness is the recognition that, just like each of us, all other beings wish for happiness and ease in their lives. In that way, our deepest wishes for ourselves and our loved ones connect us to one another. There is no difference, no separation between us at the level of our hearts. In practicing Metta, we are invited to meet every other being on that basis of inclusion. Omitting no one.

This way of seeing that recognizes the goodness within each of us is at the core of loving kindness. It's a beautiful thought, and it is closely related to the intention behind the practice of Metta. According to the Buddha, that intention is to "cultivate a limitless heart with regard to all beings" (and that, by the way, includes ourselves). A tender way of seeing each other and connecting there. As teacher Sharon Salzberg says, "knowing deeply that our lives have something to do with each other."

Loving Kindness practice is said to have originated in the time of the Buddha when he sent a group of monks into a Himalayan forest to practice meditation for three months. Initially, the nature spirits residing in the trees there tolerated the presence of the monks, but as it became clear that the monks would be with them for a while, the spirits began to make dreadful sounds at night, like tigers roaring to frighten the meditators so that they would go away. The monks became so disturbed that they became ill and could not make any progress in their meditation. Finally, the intolerable conditions led the monks to leave the forest and report their experiences to the Buddha.

As the Buddha listened to the monks, he sensed their fear as well as their ill will and anger for having been displaced. In response to their distress, As an antidote to the negative energies that had been aroused, the Buddha taught the monks this Mettā practice.

Just as a mother, with her own life,
protects her only child from hurt
So within yourself foster a limitless concern for every living creature.
Display a heart of boundless love for all the world
In all its height and depth and broad extent
Love unrestrained, without hate or enmity.
Then as you stand or walk, sit or lie,
until overcome by drowsiness
Devote your mind entirely to this,
it is known as divinely dwelling here.

Upon hearing this teaching, the monks returned to the forest, and practicing the instructions as the Buddha had taught, the whole atmosphere around them became permeated with their radiant thoughts of loving-kindness. The spirits were so affected by this power of love from that time on they allowed the monks to meditate in peace. And, as the story goes, in the peace that permeated the forest, all of the monks were then able to deepen their meditation to the point that each achieved enlightenment.

Metta was then introduced as a means for overcoming fear and negativity towards other beings by concentrating instead on intentions of unrestrained love. The assumption in engaging in this practice is that the capacity for such love is already within us; the practice is about bringing it more to the forefront, to ease access to it so that kindness is more available more automatic in our interactions with others. The practice is said to lead to a mind so saturated with goodwill that it responds uniformly to all situations with benevolence. But the origin story also points out that, as well as the capacity for unconditional love, we have within us negative responses to threats to our well-being and to our desire to have circumstances conform to our needs. These responses interfere with our innate capacity to love unrestrained and without conditions.

The Buddhist tradition names these interferences to loving kindness as the near and far enemies of a boundless heart. The far enemies are Fear and ill will. They are enemies because they disable the heart; fear closes the heart in an attempt to protect it; ill will, anger and their legion of affiliates like aversion, self-judgment, criticism, blame, contempt, etc., harden the heart and, as one teacher put it, disfigure our spirits. They are far enemies because their effects on our well-being are usually easy to identify. We recognize when we are afraid; we can tell when anger, dislike or defensiveness color our mood. In both cases, the flow of love stops.

There are also enemies of Loving Kindness that are more subtle, however. They are the near enemies that mimic love, or can be mistaken for love, or that somehow put an edge on love. Attachment is considered a near enemy because it places conditions on love; love becomes somewhat contingent on getting what "I" or the ego wants from another, whether it is reciprocal love, whether we want certain behaviors or attitudes from another; in any case, when bringing one's personal preferences into the mix, the love is no longer unconditional. And there is what Christina Feldman calls "selfish affection" that is extended to those we love but excludes those who are difficult or whom we don't know. Love then is compromised.

Expectation is another subtle version of attachment because we mix our love with our wishes for (and hope for) the other. We care, but often, our presumptions about others (think children) stem from or evolve into our dreams, our pride, and our needs rather than about others. Even the most benevolent expectations can feel like pressure and judgment to someone else. Both attachment and expectation have within them a personal agenda, which, if not met, can lead to disappointment and distancing. Love may be present in either case, but it is not unbounded.

So it is said that expectation and attachment distort unbounded love; hate and anger prevent it. Both near and far enemies color our love with personal agendas.

All this makes Metta sound like a big order, doesn't it? How do we love unconditionally with a fully open heart in the face of our vulnerabilities, protective instincts and human wants and needs? Well, we begin in the only place we can. We begin where we are.

We start with the intention to cultivate kindness. The word cultivate is important here because it implies that we can grow and expand this quality of the heart through practice. Remember that the assumption in engaging in these practices is that this quality of unbounded kindness is already within us; the intention is to bring it more to the forefront, to ease access to it so that we can strengthen our responses in our interactions with others. The intention is an invitation to incline our hearts and minds toward befriending all beings.

And then we think about and ponder upon Loving Kindness. In fact, Neuroscience has verified that Loving Kindness phrases and practice allow us to take advantage of the brain's neuroplasticity. Repetition of the phrases and of the practice carve deeper grooves in neural pathways that light up when we are experiencing connection, warmth and caring. Research has demonstrated that changes in the brain occur after only 7 weeks of daily loving-kindness practice and the circuitry that is lighted up is associated with a sense of well-being and happiness. There are other benefits of the practice that research has recorded as well, like decreased stress and enhanced social connections. The added bonus is that as the circuitry strengthens with repetition, it becomes an antidote to our human tendencies to tilt toward the negative.

It's important to note that Metta does not assume that we begin with unbounded love. Instead, we chip away at the boundaries of resistance that have arisen from previous conditioning and experiences, and as we do, more and more people, situations, emotions and sensations are included in our field of receptivity.

Neither do we have to be 'nice' nor is it required that we feel any special affection for another person to practice it. We instead are acknowledging our connection at the deepest level to other beings, that we want the same things; that there is goodness at the core. It is not about approving or liking them. This practice is more dependent on our intention and our attitude than on the feelings we have as we practice it. We are concentrating/focusing attention on our intentions toward other beings- and it is the repetition of these intentions that inclines our hearts. And, as an inclination of the heart, the effects accumulate.

There is a caveat though. We do have to practice. Repeatedly. Even when discouraged that you don't feel the 'good' feeling. When that happens, and it's likely, you bring kindness to yourself and remember the goodwill that is behind the intention. As another teacher has said- "Filling yourself up with well wishes, eventually it will spill over..."

A favorite description of Metta is that, as we practice, and the more we practice, we are creating a zone of harmlessness. Or as Ruth King phrases it:

Metta is atmospheric. It controls the climate of kindness and warmth and in doing so gradually uproots the fear and the manifestations of ill will. We create a zone of warmth, caring and kindness when we offer ourselves metta; we project those same qualities towards others when we hold the disposition of Metta in our hearts as we go about in the world. "

That atmospheric zone of harmlessness reminds me of a poem.

The Quiet Power

*I walked backwards, against time
and that's where I caught the moon,
singing at me.*

*I steeped downwards, into my seat
and that's where I caught freedom,
waiting for me, like a lilac.*

*I ended thought, and I ended story.
I stopped designing, and arguing, and
sculpting a happy life.*

I didn't die. I didn't turn to dust.

*Instead I chopped vegetables,
and made a calm lake in me
where the water was clear and sourced and still.*

*And when the ones I loved came to it,
I had something to give them, and
it offered them a soft road out of pain.*

I became beloved.

*And I came to know that this was it.
The quiet power.
I could give something mighty, lasting,
that stopped the wheel of chaos,*

*by tending to the river inside,
keeping the water rich and deep,
keeping a bench for you to visit.*

Tara Sophia Mohr

212

Including Me

An essential aspect of the Metta or Loving Kindness practice is about touching into our true nature. As teacher Pema Chodron puts it, "to first find the tenderness that we already have." Like Chodron, many Buddhist teachers tell us that this practice begins with ourselves, that unless we love ourselves, we cannot really extend a loving heart to others. In fact, it has been said that If we try to practice meditation without the foundation of goodwill towards ourselves and others, it is like trying to row across a river without first untying the boat; our efforts, no matter how strenuous, will not bear fruit.

BUT .....Even though we are instructed to direct wishes for happiness and well-being to ourselves, many of us find that we are a difficult target for loving, kind wishes. We are often more willing to soften our hearts for family members and countless other beings than we are for ourselves.

With this in mind, I conducted a brief experiment with four close friends. First, I asked these four to bring to mind one of their dear friends, a person or being for whom they felt warmth and caring, but not a family member.

Then I asked a series of questions about the person. I began by suggesting they think about one of the person's best qualities, one of the things they most liked or admired; then I asked if they let this person know that that quality is valued. Next, I suggested that they think of one of the person's annoying or more difficult characteristics and asked how they responded to that in their friend. I then asked how they responded when the person was having a difficult time and then what response they gave when something wonderful or positive happened. Lastly, I suggested they think of a time when they disagreed with the person about something, perhaps about how the person was handling a problem or a parenting issue or simply a difference of opinion. What was the response to the person then?

Once these questions were considered, I went through the same list again, but this time, I asked them to answer about themselves; that is, I asked them to think of one of their best qualities. Did they allow themselves to value that? How did they respond to one of their more difficult characteristics? And how have they responded to themselves when they have done something poorly or when they have handled a situation badly?

As you might guess, before I had even finished asking this second round of questions, each of the women became aware of discrepancies in their responses between the two sets of questions. Every one of the four recognized that they were much harder on themselves than they would be with their friend. That it was easier to be supportive and kind when it wasn't their behavior at issue. When I asked what gets in the way of offering the same thoughtfulness, kindness, and gentleness to themselves as would be offered to a friend, one mentioned that, while growing up, she was never given the message to be nice to herself but was told to always be nice to others no matter what. Another said the old patterns of inner judgment and expectations of being perfect, allowing herself no mistakes, were getting in the way.

We are so hard on ourselves. It's no wonder then that the practice of Metta presents problems for many. Issues of self-worth surface, and family and cultural conditioning interfere with a wholehearted embrace of our own well-being. Also, some say it feels too selfish, too self-indulgent, too egocentric.

Sharon Salzberg, the expert on loving kindness, writes that the most powerful insight that comes from metta practice is the sense of non-separateness from all other beings; she says that that insight comes from an open heart, one that is INCLUSIVE rather than exclusive. It is ironic, then, that often the first response that metta practice arouses is exactly the opposite: separating ourselves from others, putting ourselves in a different category, as my friends did, because we are not as deserving or as able to receive metta as are other beings.

For those of us who bring those kinds of conditioned resistances into practice, the question becomes: How can we become more able to include ourselves in the offers of kindness and to do so genuinely with sincerity and integrity?

One simple possibility is to do what one of my friends suggested. She said, "Why not extend your circle of friendships to include yourself, to treat yourself as you would treat a friend? To just be with the question, 'How would I be responding if I were my own friend?'"

Perhaps practicing this off the cushion might increase our receptiveness (open) to metta phrases on the cushion.

And remembering

We have not come here to take prisoners
or to confine our wondrous spirits
but to experience ever and ever more deeply
our divine courage, freedom and Light.
Hafiz

May we see in ourselves the tenderness that we already have and the goodness that is already there. The Zen teaching is that it takes 300,000 times.

And, as Rumi says

If your thought is a rose, you will be a rose garden.

Maybe we should think about it.

Teddy

When our dog, Teddy, was almost 13 her signs of aging were becoming more apparent. She was anxious when she didn't know where I was in the house, and she was losing her hearing. One day, I walked out of the house by the front door to pick up the mail, leaving Teddy behind as I closed the door. I returned to the house by the garage door and noticed that Teddy wasn't there to greet me as she usually did. I walked to the front of the house and saw her sitting close to the door, clearly waiting for me to return. She hadn't heard me open the back door, nor had she heard me come behind her in the hall. I stopped and just looked at her, sweetly waiting there. And my heart swelled with the poignancy of both loving this little companion and the sadness that I would one day lose her.

And then I realized that she was sitting there still anxiously waiting, that there was a degree of fear she feels, a vulnerability of sorts when I was not with her. I felt compassion for her state of being and I went to her and picked her up and cradled her for a few moments.

Later, I thought about this sequence. My first response to seeing her at the door waiting was about me: my feelings, my experience. And the fact of her aging and my wish that I could keep her just as she is. And recognizing that there was nothing I could do to make that happen. But my second response was about her experience, and there was something I could do to alleviate the anxiety she was feeling at that moment.

That movement from 'about me' to 'about her' allowed me to relieve her momentary suffering. And in that simple movement was the essence of compassion.

New York Subway
========

The beauty of people in the subway
that evening, Saturday, holding the door for whoever
was slower or
left behind

....

the young woman
holding the door for more than 3 minutes for
the feeble, stumbling, hunched little man who
could not raise his head,
whose hand I held, to
help him into the subway-car -
so we were
joined in helping him & someone
seeing us, gives up his seat,
learning
from us what we had learned from each other.

Hilda Morley

Compassion Triad

A poem about ordinary people noticing the vulnerability of a fellow human being - - the feeble, hunched little man - - then stepping in to provide some ease and contact, some connection.

We've all helped others in this way; we've all offered an arm and held open a door. Known someone who was having difficulty, and, being touched by that person's struggle, were moved to help in some way. That really is the definition of compassion: the capacity to notice suffering, to be touched by suffering and to act to relieve suffering.

It's a subject that has generated a lot of conversation and research among the social science disciplines in the last several years. One of the most prominent experts in the field today is Paul Gilbert, author of The Compassionate Mind. He describes three ways we can experience compassion, each from a somewhat different perspective: the compassion that we give to others, the compassion that we receive from others, and the compassion that we give to ourselves.

The first of these is represented by the poem at the head of this page: compassion is an experience that we feel and express towards others, responding to the suffering of another human being.

Compassion is, in this sense, simply a response to the human condition that suffering is a reality of life and that everyone struggles at some time. In experiencing compassion, we are allowing the world to touch us; we remember that we are a part of the universal story that everyone wants to be happy and well and safe and free from suffering, just as we do. Compassion connects us; it is a recognition of our belonging, as Mary Oliver would say- "in the family of things." As those helpers on the New York subway connected with one another in their response to suffering, they became a part of that family. This is compassion that we feel and express towards others.

Paul Gilbert says that If we learn to concentrate our attention, thoughts and behaviors on compassion if we imagine ourselves as compassionate and think about how we have been compassionate to others, we stimulate brain activity that creates feelings of peacefulness, calmness and connectedness as well as giving us insight into the nature of our role in the flow and family of life. We are thus offering ourselves a gift of belonging as we focus on offering the gift of compassion to others.

The second experience of compassion is compassion that is directed towards ourselves from others, the compassion that we receive. Parker Palmer, author, poet and wise elder, has often shared his struggle with clinical depression in his writing. Here, he describes his experience of receiving compassion during one of his depressive episodes.

There was a friend who came to me, after asking permission to do so, every afternoon at about 4 o'clock, sat me down in a chair in the living room, took off my shoes and socks and massaged my feet. He hardly ever said anything, and yet, out of his intuitive sense, he, from time to time, would say a very brief word like, "I can feel your struggle today" or, farther down the road, "I feel that you're a little stronger at this moment and I'm glad for that." But beyond that, he would say hardly anything. He would give no advice.

Somehow, he found that one place in my body, namely the soles of my feet, where I could experience some sort of connection to another human being. And the act of massaging just, you know, in a way that I really don't have words for, kept me connected with the human race.

What he mainly did for me, of course, was to be willing to be present to me in my suffering.

This is such a beautiful story for several reasons. First, the humble nature of the act of compassion, massaging Palmer's feet. It is not a grand gesture but such a touching human one. The friend, while offering his presence, his time, and his attunement to Palmer's state of being, asked nothing of Palmer. And because of Palmer's willingness to receive his friend's compassionate offering, Palmer was able to feel their mutual humanity. He remained connected to life instead of isolated and alone.

For many of us, though, this experience of compassion can be challenging because the vulnerability we are recognizing, the suffering that is the object of compassion, is our own.

There is often a reluctance when in the place of vulnerability; whether the vulnerability stems from physical pain, from sadness about a loss, or from fear, there may be an urge to turn away from gestures of kindness rather than accept so much goodness...

I know that for me when, years ago, I had been diagnosed and then was recovering from a significant illness. I found that I had to be intentional in my practice about maintaining an open heart in order to take in the well-wishes that were sent to me. The compassion that came toward me then seemed to flood my heart in a way that felt unfamiliar and almost overwhelming. Staying open meant that I had to create internal space in my meditation by first allowing the difficult energies aroused by the diagnosis to course through me so that there was room for the love to come in.

Each of these examples, the poem, Palmer's story, and my experience illustrate that compassion is, by its nature, relational. It has to do with how we relate to the world we live in, to our fellow human beings, and to ourselves. It is how love responds to suffering in others or to the suffering in ourselves. It's also important to note that when we give and receive compassion, we are cultivating a stance of approaching the difficulties in life rather than avoiding those experiences. We are not denying or distracting ourselves from the realities of this human existence, and by assuming this stance of approach, we are at the same time cultivating confidence in our ability to meet whatever circumstances come our way, as well as cultivating the resilience to bounce back from setbacks. This is the sense in which compassion is tough and sometimes gritty, arising from the strength to be with unpleasant events and move through them to be able to offer a wise response...

The third of the compassion experiences that Gilbert mentions is that of directing compassion towards ourselves. Of the three experiences of compassion, perhaps this is the most difficult of all. We in the West are a culture of self-critics. We feel as if we don't deserve kindness when we screw up. We believe that being tough on ourselves is a reliable motivator. But what is being revealed in studies of self-compassion is that self-compassion serves as a powerful antidote to self-criticism and perfectionistic thinking; research suggests that self-compassionate people bounce back more easily from setbacks and are more likely to learn from mistakes. Not only that, there is good evidence that practicing self-compassion leads to more happiness, optimism and better relationships with others.

While we may have heard that we cannot be truly compassionate with others unless we are compassionate with ourselves, as research has discovered, that is really not true. But even though self-compassion may not be a prerequisite for compassion and wisdom, it IS a way to help ensure that we have the strength and sustenance we need to make a difference for others over the long term.

While it is increasingly evident that our human natures have evolved to be caring and compassionate, just because compassion is already in us doesn't mean it is the default response of our nervous system. Flight, fright or flee can easily trump compassion unless we work to develop and strengthen our capacities for seeing clearly and for being able to be with suffering, the turning toward the realities of life that mindfulness cultivates.

Richard Rohr, a Franciscan priest, writes

The True Self does not teach us compassion as much as [the true self] is compassion already. And from this more spacious and grounded place, one naturally connects, empathizes, forgives and loves just about everything.....Yet, it still must be awakened and chosen.

Because they are based on research evidence of their effectiveness, we know that the practices taught in the self-compassion and cultivating compassion programs offered on many retreats and by many teachers can develop and strengthen those capacities. And there is good neurological news about the effects of compassionate actions. Research has discovered that the same circuits in our brains that light up when we are holding a baby, light up when making a gesture of compassion. Compassionate actions are associated with the affiliative networks in the brain: the connecting networks. Those pathways are similar to those activated by feelings of love.

So, three experiences of compassion: we experience compassion when we respond to the suffering of another, we experience compassion directed toward ourselves from others, and we can direct compassion to ourselves in times of struggle. Whenever we allow ourselves to be touched by human distress, our own or someone else's, when we open our hearts to pain and suffering, when we act to relieve that distress, we are coming from the place of goodness that is within each of us, that is within all human beings.

We are cultivating a loving nature, and within us, we are stimulating evolved cognitive capacities. Through our practice and in our actions, we can intend compassion to become more of a verb.

Joy needs space and room to emerge.
Christina Feldman

In the last 30 years, there have been 46,000 scientific papers just on depression and an underwhelming 400 on joy.

Joy

If Joy needs space and room to emerge, as Christina Feldman asserts, how can it possibly reveal itself if it receives as little attention as the statistics suggest: outnumbered 115 to 1 in the science realm? Fortunately, teacher Tara Brach claims that "we can wake up the lens of Joy." Let's consider some ways that we can do that.

Poet Mary Oliver has a suggestion.

<u>Snow Geese</u>

*One fall day I heard
above me, and above the sting of the wind, a sound
I did not know, and my look shot upward; it was
a flock of snow geese, winging it
faster that the ones we usually see,
and, being the color of snow, catching the sun
so they were, in part at least, golden. I
held my breath
as we do
sometimes
to stop time
when something wonderful
has touched us...
The geese
flew on.
I have never seen them again.
Maybe I will, someday, somewhere.
Maybe I won't.
It doesn't matter.
What matters
is that, when I saw them,
I saw them as through the veil,
secretly, joyfully, clearly.*

The poet 'held her breath as we do sometimes,' creating a pause so that she could be fully present in her experience of joy. As she did on that fall day, we can wake up the lens of joy by noticing and stopping when we hear a summons, whether the call of geese, a dog's cheerful bark or a child's laughter.

And the poet also gives us another hint about waking up through the lens of Joy. Her words: "stop time when something wonderful has touched you," add to the notion of pausing by suggesting that we savor that experience, that we feel in our bodies the touch of something wonderful to help us become more familiar with how the taste of joy lives within us.

Sharing our joyful moments is one way to savor them to familiarize ourselves with the sensations of joy. I am reminded of a story that a friend told a group of us not long ago. She, a grandmother, was hosting her family for a celebratory dinner. As one of her granddaughters was engaged with the serious task of drawing, my friend stood quietly behind her, observing this much-loved child creating her art. Then, turning away to tend to something in the kitchen, my friend heard her grandchild say, "Grandma, don't leave. I need your help watching me!" In her re-telling of this sweet moment, not only did my friend have an opportunity to re-experience "something wonderful touching her," but each of us listening felt - - experienced - - a moment of joy for her. My friend savored and spread her joy.

This experience for each of us listening to our friend, our feeling of happiness for her happiness, is an example of what in the Buddhist tradition would be called appreciative Joy. Appreciative Joy is considered a quality of the awakened heart, a capacity within every one of us. It is responding to the Joy of another with the wish that their happiness continue, that it multiply.

There is a formal meditation practice, mudita meditation, for cultivating this quality. The formal practice of Joy is much like the practice of loving-kindness: formulate phrases to say silently to ourselves and then offer those wishes to an ever-widening circle. Sample phrases might be:

May my/your happiness continue.

May you know more moments of Joy.

May your Joy multiply.

May you savor these moments.

We can practice mudita meditation by holding someone clearly in our minds, visualizing them at a time we knew they were happy, acknowledging all the good things in their life, and then repeating one of the phrases, like "May your happiness continue, may it increase." AND...It can be interesting to note what happens as we engage in this. Often, feelings of envy can arise, even if we're sending these wishes to someone we care deeply about. In the practice of muditata, then, we learn more about our mind's habits, and we can, at the same time, shift in the direction of inclining ourselves toward the lens of Joy. In fact, one writer called embracing Joy a 'moral obligation;' I think he was referring to the infectious nature of Joy - - how it infects the atmosphere and touches the hearts of anyone in its vicinity, as it did mine when our friend shared her story.

But too often, we back away from sharing Joy. Maybe because we fear that others will think we're elevating ourselves, or maybe because we're afraid we don't deserve it when so many others here and around the world are suffering. Here's what poet David Budbill says about that.

> *...when we walk in the woods every evening over fallen leaves,*
> *through yellow light when nights are cool, and days warm,*
> *when I am so happy I am afraid I might explode or disappear*
> *or somehow be taken away from all this,*
> *at those times when I feel so happy, so good, so alive, so in love with*
> *the world, with my own sensuous, beautiful life, suddenly*
>
> *I think about all the suffering and pain in the world, the agony*
> *and dying. I think about all those people being tortured, right now,*
> *in my name. But I still feel happy and good, alive and in love with*
> *the world and with my lucky, guilty, sensuous, beautiful life because,*
>
> *I know in the next minute or tomorrow all this may be*
> *taken from me, and therefore I've got to say, right now*
> *what I feel and know and see, I've got to say, right now,*
> *how beautiful and sweet this world can be.*

Noticing, recognizing and pausing to acknowledge moments of Joy, whether our own Joy or the Joy and happiness we see in others and then savoring and sharing those moments, spreading Joy, these can help wake up our lens of Joy.

Finally, we can cultivate Joy through forming intentions around it. My dogs, Brady and Teddy, were helpful every morning in reminding me to intend Joy. After they ate their breakfast, both dogs would come to either side of my chair (where I was reading the paper); Brady pawed me, and Teddy jumped up to tell me that it was time for our daily ceremony. I then got up with them bouncing at my heels, walked to the space in our kitchen where there is some floor room and I said," Show me what you got today." Brady began to twirl (I counted 4 times as I made a circle with my hand), and Teddy jumped as high off the floor as she could and then touched her nose to the refrigerator. I applauded, told them that those were show-stopping tricks and then led them to the pantry where Brady twirled one more time, and Teddy jumped up again; I opened the treat bag and gave them one bacon strip each. Every day - - same routine. It never failed to leave me smiling. Their enthusiasm, as if the treat they were about to get was the most wonderful thing in the world, and to them on any particular day it was; and I was reminded by their Joy to notice Joy during the day.

Opening to, answering Joy's summons, savoring and sharing, cultivating and intending - - all ways to wake up the lens of Joy.

Mary Oliver And Joy

Rick Hanson, a neuropsychologist and meditation/mindfulness teacher, tells us that our brains are structured in a way that they are velcro for latching on to our difficult experiences but Teflon for the pleasures; our tough moments are much more likely to become embedded in our memories than our pleasant ones. Because of that bias of our brains, he says that we can, and we must, learn to savor our experiences of joy and happiness, to spend time enough with them so that they get into our neuro-circuitry. This seems to be a practice that Mary instinctively followed. And found delight as she did so.

<u>At Blackwater Pond</u>

At Blackwater Pond the tossed waters have settled
after a night of rain.
I dip my cupped hands. I drink
a long time. It tastes
like stone, leaves, fire. It falls cold
into my body, waking the bones. I hear them
deep inside me, whispering
oh what is that beautiful thing
that just happened?`
Mary Oliver

She allowed this experience literally to enter her, drinking a long time, naming the tastes, following the water into her body, and "waking the bones" deep inside. She welcomed it. She embodied it, and she savored "the beautiful thing that just happened."

She has also offered us instructions about such moments. And that's what I think they are. They are more than suggestions. They are imperative instructions.

If you suddenly and unexpectedly feel joy, **don't hesitate… Give in to it.** *(And we need to do this because) There are plenty of lives and whole towns destroyed or about to be. We are not wise and not very often kind. And much can never be redeemed. So don't be afraid of its plenty.* **Joy is not made to be a crumb.**
Mary Oliver

James Baraz, a mindfulness and meditation teacher, has created a 10-month program titled Awakening Joy. He notes that Joy is saying "yes" to life, no matter what. It is experiencing our aliveness right here in this human body. Like Oliver's "waking her bones with the cold water of Blackwater Pond."

But we have to be present to experience it.

The mindfulness perspective contends that we often override our innate capacity for joy with our incessant inner dialogue and our tendency to grasp the next thing rather than experience what is right here in the present moment. We also get so easily lost in habitual behaviors that we miss the opportunities to notice and celebrate the small moments of joy in life.

Mary Oliver, fortunately, more mindful than that, was present when "something wonderful touched her" at the sight of the snow geese; she welcomed the grasshopper eating sugar out of her hand; and, because such moments are so available in the world, she begs us "not to walk by without pausing" so that we can experience them.

What good advice that seems- to "not walk by without pausing"- adding more intentional pauses to our day pauses that allow us to notice what is around us, pauses that give us the opportunity to be present for 'something wonderful.'

Equanimity And Mom

In April, 1968, the night before he was assassinated in Memphis, Tennessee, Martin Luther King Jr. spoke these famous words at the end of his speech:

Well, I don't know what will happen now. We've got some difficult days ahead. But it doesn't matter with me now. Because I've been to the mountaintop… And I'm happy tonight. I'm not worried about anything. I'm not fearing any man.

King's life and those of Gandhi, Thich Nhat Hanh and the Dalai Lama exemplify the ability to be steadfast in the face of unimaginable threats. And while none of us may ever face such serious threats to our very safety, we all have or will face difficulties in this life: the sadness of losing our loved ones, the diminishments of our own aging and illnesses, the many ups and downs, gains and losses, pleasures and pains, that we experience as we make our way in the world. Buddhist teachings name these fluctuations and shifts of circumstances that each of us will experience as the vicissitudes of life. The instability, the unpredictability. It may be a home lost to a hurricane or an automobile accident resulting in serious injury or a random act of violence. The vicissitudes include positive experiences as well as successes and pleasures, which are as subject to instability and change as are the negatives. And though we may want to be in charge of how life treats us and add as many of positive experiences as we can, conditions are always changing.

The brahmavihara of equanimity is about an internal ability to be clear in mind and balanced in response to these inevitable challenges.

We can fairly easily get an idea of what is meant by the other three immeasurables. We all have some knowledge of love, and we all have known kindness. I think the same is true for compassion and joy. We have some experience with them. Equanimity, though, is not so much a part of our everyday vocabulary. In fact, one teacher has described equanimity as counter-cultural because it requires a quality of stillness, non-reactivity, of patience. It is not about doing, about being busy, about taking over or being in charge of anything. It is about being with what is from a state of deep acceptance; it is about navigating life's ever-changing conditions, those highs and lows, the 10,000 sorrows and 10,000 joys, with a calm understanding. We only have to think about the three years with COVID-19 to be reminded of life's shifting circumstances and our lack of control over external events.

Equanimity is about remaining internally steadfast and spacious in the face of such challenges. Being with 'what is' with a balanced steadiness. There is an element of resilience in equanimity. Just as a bamboo tree can be buffeted and bent by strong winds and heavy rain, bowing to the experiences of life without breaking and then returning to being upright once the storm has passed, similarly equanimity enables us to withstand both the good and fierce weather of our experiences without holding tightly to what cannot last and with the strength to rebound from hardships.

Perspective is a requisite of equanimity. Seeing clearly a bigger picture of events, about having been to the mountaintop like Dr. King. As mindfulness practitioners, we often talk about the "Pause" between stimulus and response, giving ourselves a moment between an event and reacting to that event. Giving ourselves some space to consider what might be appropriate to do or say in a situation. But the heart quality of equanimity requires Space, with a capital S, a space much more open and vast than the space of the moment or the pause. The space of perspective is the space that takes in the whole of the circumstance, both internal and external, as well as the space that may include beyond what is present in the moment. It is the space of clear seeing, the heart quality most associated with wisdom. Equanimity brings discernment and understanding into the heart; it protects against the attachment that can make loving kindness sticky; it protects compassion from spilling into overwhelm and protects joy from exaggerating into giddiness...

Equanimity also includes the quality of patience. A Taoist quote asks, "Do you have the patience to wait til the mud settles and the water is clear? Can you remain unmoving til the right action arises by itself?" Equanimity involves the ability to wait, to stay with an experience, especially a difficult, disorienting one, long enough to reach some clarity about the best course of action to take.

When spaciousness pairs with patience, the opportunity is created for other possibilities to emerge. I have experienced the gift of this equanimous pairing of spaciousness and patience, and it served me when my mother was living her final days.

On the Wednesday before Mom died, she had become quite restless - - still conscious of her surroundings during the day but more agitated. We had arranged for Hospice that afternoon, and I had requested that they make sure Mom was given something to help her sleep. As evening came and her aide was scheduled to leave at 8:00, it was evident to me that I needed to stay with her that night; she was too restless to be left alone, so I settled myself in a chair in Mom's room.

The drug protocol hadn't yet been initiated, and her agitation by that time had increased to the point that she was attempting to get out of bed every 10 - 15 minutes. She was unable to stop herself from these attempts and she was not hearing or responding to anything I would say to her.

For the next few hours and several times an hour, I witnessed her struggle to move to the edge of the bed. She couldn't sit up on her own, but she would reach her arms toward me in what seemed like a plea to help her up. Then as gently as I could, I would reposition her on the bed. Repeating this over and over was hard work for each of us. And despite the drugs having been started at 9:00 pm, her unrest continued.

Finally, at one point between these dances that we were doing, I left her bedroom and collapsed on the living room sofa - - and just breathed for a few minutes. These breaths, these few minutes, were for me. These were the moments that I needed to settle myself. It was not until then that I remembered to give myself permission to practice self-compassion. The compassion I felt for my Mom had been almost automatic and conscious, but I had been so concentrated on her I had not been aware of what was going on within me. So, I allowed myself to feel my body's weariness. I began to register the sadness in my heart, to admit my frustration with being unable to ease her discomfort. I finally gave myself the gift of opening to my own experience. And as I sat there,

I also became aware of how spent and exhausted my mother must be. Her old body had been struggling in this way for hours.

Though I wasn't conscious of this thought or feeling then, as I've reflected on this moment, it seemed as if I received a wordless awareness, an awareness that my mother and I were together in this unrepeatable experience, just the two of us. That what was happening was simply a part of things and that there was nothing to do but surrender to it.

And with that, I went back to be with my mother. I lay down next to her on the bed and put my arm through hers so that as she began to move toward the edges of the bed, I could hold her next to me and quietly speak to her. After a while, we both fell asleep, and when I awoke later, the drugs had taken effect, and she was not restless again. Her peaceful death followed two days later.

Teacher Christina Feldman describes equanimity this way:

It is not developed in the most sublime and peaceful moments in our lives but in the moments we feel most shattered, most lost and unbalanced.

And - - so it was for me.

I had to let go of concentrating on her moments of agitation and let go of my wanting those to stop. I needed to sense into my own state of being in order to allow and be open to the greater whole of the experience that was happening to each of us. In allowing myself to yield to the full reality of the moment, the way to a rare and sacred circumstance was then revealed.

I've later heard equanimity described as a greater spaciousness that allows. It is 'greater' because it is more than the space of a pause. It is not bound by time. It is an open space without edges, one that includes life's joys and sorrows, triumphs and losses all at once - - leaving nothing out. It is being and living in that space and celebrating and grieving events, all the while remaining receptive to life.

And I've come to see that in that spaciousness is love. It is the yielding of control and the acceptance of things as they are. The wisdom of understanding that there are things that can not be 'fixed' and moments when all there is to do is to be with and in that moment.

End Note

Now that we know our brains are plastic and now that there is evidence that mindfulness and meditation lead to positive changes in the brain, it almost feels obligatory to engage in those practices that lead to greater well-being for ourselves and, importantly, that actually can contribute to growing a calmer, more sane world. We have the provable means to affect our consciousness, to shift our brains in the direction of more compassion and kindness, and to cultivate our capacities for more inclusivity and considered responses. And as we do this work, we are changing the air (the narrative) around us. We infuse the culture with a healthier attitude.

Gil Fronsdal described equanimity as a deep love almost synonymous with peace. And as a choice to connect to something that is already here within us. In fact, he raises the question about all of the Brahmaviharas: are they emotions? or attitudes? Or motivations? Or are they decisions, choices we make as we encounter and engage in the world?

> *Loving Kindness as a decision to befriend, to connect rather than separate*
> *Compassion as a decision to care about and respond to suffering rather than pity*
> *Appreciative Joy as a decision to celebrate the joy and beauty in the world rather than focus on what is lacking in our lives*
> *Equanimity as a decision to allow rather than control*
>
> Gil Fronsdal

We can make a decision - - a choice - - and our heart will be glad.

Acknowledgements

There are now many inspiring teachers of mindfulness and meditation. Some are ancient, like the Buddha; others are newer on the scene. I was fortunate to discover my primary teachers after I had begun listening to Sharon Salzberg and Joseph Goldstein on tape in the 1990's. Those two drew me to attend a Tricycle: A Buddhist Review conference in New York in 2001. It was there that I had a chance to sit with Tara Brach; it is Tara's grace and embodiment of the dharma that have been a sustaining influence on me since. Because of that fortuitous experience with her, I began to attend retreats she led through the Insight Meditation Community of Washington. Then, in 2011, she, along with Pat Coffee, Hugh Byrne and Jonathan Foust began a two-year teacher training program that included monthly, in person, weekend sessions in D.C. These four wonderful teachers provided not only a philosophical and educational foundation for this material, but were inspiring role models of authenticity and kindness. I am so grateful to each. Thank you.

I also want to mention a teacher I have never met but whose gentle manner and wise dharma have been important to my study and practice. Gil Fronsdal offers his teachings from his sangha in Redwood City, California on audio.dharma.org. I have found his talks to be an especially valuable resource in sustaining my personal practice.

As I've worked on this book, I've had encouragement, a bit of badgering and lots of support from important people in my life.

My first readers trudged through a disorganized, unedited version of these pages. I can't thank them enough for their uncomplaining willingness to do this favor. Their comments have been helpful, their thoroughness appreciated, and their contributions valuable. These special people - - Peggy, Kristina, Sandra, Jane, Barbara, Lisa, Joan and Spud - - were and are the wind behind my back. (I cannot give myself wings!!!!)

Matt, my son, was also a first reader. I began this project because I wanted to leave him something tangible of me. He has always been a light in my life. What he thinks of this has mattered a lot. I needed to receive his approval.

And finally, Philip. Without his unwavering belief, hours of attention to the manuscript, and even more hours of conversation about this book and mindfulness and meditation in general, the book would not exist. His dedication to making this happen for me personifies love.

References for Quotations and Poems

P3   "The essential human calling……." John Wellwood
johnwellwood.com

P11   "In Any Event"   Dorianne Laux   Only As The Day Is Long: New and Selected Poems

P13   "Do not go by revelation…."   The Buddha   Karaniya Metta Sutta

P17   "the witchery of living"   Mary Oliver   Evidence: Poems

P19   "When something is of us……"   James Hollis   What Matters Most

P20   "is the surest way……"   James Hollis   What Matters Most

P21   "The Dakini Speaks"   Jennifer Wellwood   jennifer.wellwood.com

P24   "I've been smoking…"   Unattributed

P26   "we allow……."   Ruth King   "Mindful of Race"

P27   "I can be miserable……"   Toni Morrison   Home

P27   "Unconditional"   Jennifer Wellwood   jenniferwellwood.com

P28   "However solid things may appear on the surface…"   Sharon Salzberg   Faith: Trusting Your Own Deepest Experience

P29   "It takes humility……"   Adam Grant   Think Again

P31   "Yes"   William Stafford   The Way It Is: New and Selected Poems

P35   "Ambiguity"   Rilke   Letters To A Young Poet

P36   "A human being is a universe of experience,…"A.H. Almas   Spacecruiser Inquiry: True Guidance for the Inner Journey (Diamond Body Series, 1)

P42   "A wolf in me……."   Carl Sandburg   poetryfoundation.org

P43   "We are the culmination of 13 billion years of evolution….."Walter Truet Anderson The Next Enlightenment: Integrating East and West in a New Vision of Human Evolution

P46   "We begin life with the world presenting itself to us……"   Sidney Jourard The Transparent Self: Self-disclosure and Well-being

P49   hypnotic spell, so -- Sidney Jourard ---**Missing**

P51   "To allow oneself to be carried away……."   Thomas Merton Conjectures of a Guilty Bystander

P52 "Awareness is the primary currency of the human condition…….."
Andrew Olendzki "Busy Signal," Tricycle magazine Winter 2009

P54   "…the challenge is twofold: first, to bring awareness……"   Jon
Kabat-Zinn Coming To Our Senses

P52 "Awareness……." John Austin Mindful Poetry cih.ucsd.edu

P55   "There is a force within you that gives you life…." Rumi
quotemaster.org

P60   "What if we actually believed that this hidden wholeness…….Wayne
Muller" Sabbath Rest : Restoring the Sacred Rhythm of Rest

P61   "This being human is a guest house…" Rumi
mindfulnessassociation.net

P63   "The very act of stopping, of nurturing moments of non-doing……"
Jon Kabat-Zinn Coming To Our Senses

P66 "The most difficult of all possible tasks is to come to understand one's
own mind." Joseph Goldstein   Insight Meditation: The Practice of
Freedom

P71   "Eyesight" Archie Randolph Ammons poetrynook.com

P73 "We don't sit in meditation to become good meditators….." Pema
Chodron Comfortable with Uncertainty: 108 Teachings on Cultivating
Fearlessness and Compassion

P76 "Work on becoming a native of mind, a native of heart. No
thought…." Teddy Macker A Poem for my Daughter

P84 "The ache for home lives in all of us……." Maya Angelou
goodreads.com Maya Angelou quotes

P86 "Go In and In" Danna Faulds Go In and In

P87,88 "Otherwise" Jane Kenyon Jane Kenyon: Collected Poems

P94 "Our life force may not require us to strengthen it…."   Rachel
Naomi Remen Kitchen Table Wisdom

P96 "The difficult things provoke all your irritations……" Pema Chodron
A-Z Quotes.com

P100 "Allow" Danna Faulds   Go In and In

P100   "George got stung……."   Shel Silverstein Falling Up

P108 "love without power is sentimental and anemic….."   Martin
Luther King jr The Autobiography of Martin Luther King, Jr

P105 "In healing ourselves, our wound becomes our gift........" Adam Kahane <u>Power and Love: A Theory and Practice of Social Change</u>

P111"...when we let our own light shine, we unconsciously give......." Marianne Williamson <u>Return to Love</u>

P115 "When you meet your friend on the roadside..." Kahlil Gibran <u>On Talking poets.org</u>

P123 "Knowing when to step back in the face of suffering......" Christina Feldman: <u>Boundless Heart</u>

P125 "Sometimes" David Budbill <u>Happy Life</u>

P127 "Trough" Judy Brown <u>ayearofbeinghere.com</u> 2013

P128 "We should learn to ask, "What's not wrong?" and be in touch with that." Thich Nhật Hanh <u>Peace Is Every Step: The Path of Mindfulness in Everyday Life</u>

P128 "Being in a slump is never much fun......." Dr Seuss <u>Oh The Places You'll Go</u>

P130 "You are a divine elephant........" Hafiz <u>ayearofbeinghere.com</u>

P132 "Forget about enlightenment..." John Wellwood <u>mindfulnessassociation.net</u>

P133 "There was that one hour sometime......." Joyce Sutphen <u>The Book of Hours</u>

P137 "Going to Walden" Mary Oliver <u>Devotions: Selected Poems of Mary Oliver</u>

P139 "Pulling me close.........." Rachel Remen <u>My Grandfather's Blessings</u>

P140 "Not-doing, having no urgent plans, we dawdle....." John Tarrant <u>The Light Inside the Dark</u>

P141 "I find that the deepest threat on the spiritual path is any sense..."Cynthia Bourgeault <u>The Wisdom Way of Knowing: Reclaiming An Ancient Tradition to Awaken the Heart</u>

P142 "Do you think today is just another day in your life?........" Brother David Steindl-Rast. <u>A Film: A Grateful Day with Brother David Steindal-Rast</u> Available on YouTube

P143,144 "Be Glad Your Nose Is On Your Face" Jack Perlutsky <u>poemhunter.com</u>

P145 All of the quotes on this page can be found in A Collection of Poems
By Yunus Emre   http://en.wikipedia.org/wiki/Yunus_Emre

P146 "Consider these stanzas"   Warsan Shire   verse.press

P146 "stop asking……." Julia Fehrenbacher   juliafehrenbacher.com

P147 "I pause in this moment……" David Budbill   While We've Still
Got Feet: New Poems

P148 "The real voyage of discovery…….."   Marcel Proust   La
Prisonnière the fifth volume of 'Remembrance of Things Past'

P151 "If we are honest, and if we look back at the past with an impartial
eye……"Harry R. Moody   The Five Stages of the Soul: Charting the
Spiritual Passages That Shape Our Lives

P151   "With mindfulness of mental states, we can choose….."   Jack
Kornfield   No Time Like the Present: Finding Freedom, Love, and Joy
Right Where You Are

P153 "A Brief for The Defense" Jack Gilbert Poemhunter.com: Friday,
May 4, 2012

P154 "for the last 50 years of the 20th century……"Martin Seligman

P154 "This is because…….."   Martin Seligman   Annual Meeting of the
American Psychological Association 1998; President's Address

P158 "Ninety is just fine with me" Selma Missing

P160 "If the moon only came out once a month" Cathy Ross
ayearofbeinghere.com 2013

P160   "Foolishness? No It's Not" Mary Oliver A Thousand Mornings

P162 "The range of what we think and do……" R.D. Laing

R.D. Laing Quotes on quotes.net. Nov. 16, 2023

P164 "If I walk out into the world ………" Mary Oliver Blue Horses

P167 "In the beginner's mind….." Suzuki Rochi   Zen Mind, Beginner's
Mind

P166 "Having an accurate perception of reality is not…..Andrew Newberg
Words Can Change Your Brain

P166 Goodbye Missing

P163 "Not knowing does not mean……" Suzuki Rochi Zen Mind,
Beginner's Mind

P163   "Everyone thinks he knows what a lettuce looks…."Frederick Franck The Zen of Seeing: Seeing/Drawing as Meditation

P163   "A mind is like a parachute….."   Frank Zappa Musician

P166   "When talking with another person, bring your attention to……." Ronald Siegel The Extraordinary Gift of Being Ordinary: Finding Happiness Right Where You Are

P167   "Not knowing does not mean you don't know…." Suzuki Roshi Zen Mind, Beginner's Mind

P171   "You must have a room or a certain hour of the day…."   Joseph Campbell The Power of Myth

P173   "Acceptance is about the relationship…" Bhavana Society of West Virginia; posted on the walls

P177 "The dream of my life……"   Mary Oliver   New and Selected Poems

P179 "What I want to say is…."   Mary Oliver   Red Bird: Poems by Mary Oliver

P184   "It's as if the world was given a rest…".   David Whyte   Three Sundays in November, 2020; conversations with David Whyte

P184   "…you aren't doing anything…."   Jane Hirshfield   "Fooling with Words: A Celebration of Poets and Their Craft, Bill Moyers

P186 "The Peace of Wild Things"   Wendell Berry The Peace of Wild Things

P189   "A Spiritual Journey"   Wendell Berry   The Collected Poems of Wendell Berry

P190   "What if our religion was each other……" Ganga White www.whitelotus.org>articles>rainforest-poem

P191   "I would say that there……"Mary Oliver   Upstream: Selected Essays

P192   "Wisdom and Love are the two great wings…"   Joseph Goldstein Insight Meditation: A Psychology of Freedom

P197   "You mustn't be frightened…."   Rilke   Letters to a Young Poet

P197 "The work becomes that of making an accurate inlet……"Mark Nepo The Book of Awakening: Having the Life You Want by Being Present to the Life You Have (20th Anniversary Edition)

P201   "Seeing with eyes of wholeness means recognizing……"Jon Kabat-Zinn Coming to Our Senses

P202   "The Moth, The Mountain, The Rivers" Mary Oliver A Thousand Mornings

P204 "It is not given to us to know ……" Clarissa Pinkola Estes Soul On Deck

P204 "So, despite troubling politics and despite personal challenges…" Sharon Salzberg   Faith: Trusting Your Own Deepest Experience

P207 "The Scent of Love" Llewellyen Vaughan-Lee The Bond with the Beloved

P209 "Just as a mother……" the Buddha Karaniya Metta Sutta

P212 "Metta is atmospheric……" Ruth King Mindful of Race

P212 "The Quiet Power" Tara Sophia Mohr taramohr.com

P215 "And Remembering" Hafiz xxx 2011

P215 "If your thought is a rose garden……." Rumi quotemaster.org

P217 "New York Subway" Hilda Morley To Hold My Hand: Selected Poems

P221   "The True Self……" Richard Rohr, Homilies by Fr. Richard Rohr, OFM by Center for Action and Contemplation

P222 "Joy needs space and room to emerge…" Christina Feldman Boundless Heart

P222 "Snow Geese" Mary Oliver New and Selected Poems

P224 "…when we walk in the woods…." David Budbill Happy Life

P226 "At Blackwater Pond" Mary Oliver New and Selected Poems

P226 "if you suddenly and unexpectedly……." Mary Oliver

Don't Hesitate in Swan: Poems and Prose Poems

P228 "Well, I don't know what will happen now…" Martin Luther King Jr YouTube: Martin Luther King's Last Speech: I've Been to the Mountaintop

P231 "It is not developed in the most sublime……" Christina Feldman Boundless Heart

P233 "Loving Kindness as a decision to befriend…" Gil Fronsdal

The Brahmaviharas: Introduction; Gil Fronsdal on AudioDharma; September 9, 2014

About The Author

Kay M. Davidson

Kay's experiences as a clinical psychologist and her interest in Buddhist art led her to the practice and teaching of mindfulness and meditation more than 25 years ago.

Following that initial interest, she has studied, taught and written about this journey toward becoming more awake to life.

She has been married for more than 55 years, is a mother, a grandmother and a dog lover. She has lived in Richmond, VA since 1970.

Made in the USA
Middletown, DE
26 September 2024